Praise for

The *Wisdom* Collection

This book brings together insights from some of my absolute favorite minds—the kind of people who actually walk their talk. If you're looking for real insight without the fluff, this is your book. It's like a wisdom buffet—load up your plate.
—**Oonagh Duncan, author of** *Healthy As Fck**

In a culture obsessed with quick fixes and surface solutions, *The Wisdom Collection* is a breath of fresh air. These stories are sincere, layered, and unafraid to name the full complexity of being human. They remind us that real wisdom doesn't arrive all at once—it's earned through experience, humility, and honest reflection. This book is an antidote to the noise, a meaningful companion for anyone seeking clarity, courage, and connection in uncertain times.
—**Emma Johnston, co-founder of The Reconnected and author of** *Reconnected Parenting*

As someone who has read countless business and self-help books, *The Wisdom Collective* is refreshingly different. Ann Sheybani writes one chapter (possibly my favorite) and has curated the remarkable stories of eighteen other amazing authors who articulate their life lessons on topics such as grief, risk-taking, and forgiveness. Each chapter left me wanting more, and I plan to follow up with several of the authors—which is easy to do with QR codes and information about each author following

their respective chapters. This anthology is a must-read for anyone who wants to live a happier and more fulfilling life.
—Mary Barbera, PhD, RN, BCBA-D, and bestselling author of *Turn Autism Around*

Hard-earned insights remind us that it's okay to be imperfect. Essential reading for anyone feeling overwhelmed by life's expectations.
—Cecilia and Jason Hilkey, co-founders of Happily Family, #1 international bestselling authors of *The Perfectly Imperfect Family*

Having spent decades in executive roles and now coaching leaders at the highest levels, I've learned that true leadership isn't built on frameworks or formulas—it's forged through wisdom earned in the crucible of real experience. *The Wisdom Collection* offers something increasingly rare: authentic insights from those who've navigated the messy realities of leading through uncertainty, making tough decisions with incomplete information, and building sustainable success while remaining human.
—May Busch, executive coach, author, and former COO of Morgan Stanley Europe

The Wisdom Collection is more than just a book; it is a profound and calming conversation with individuals whose experiences can inspire you to lead a better life. The stories delve deep, speaking to your soul and reminding you that life's challenges offer opportunities for learning and growth, helping you become your true self. As you read the table of contents, you will be captivated and moved by the authenticity and empathy of these leaders and their raw honesty. This book serves as a beacon, guiding you away from a noisy world and connecting you to a safe harbor of inspiration and courage. Yes, it will transform you, and that is the remarkable essence of *The Wisdom Collection*.

—Michael Feeley, career and life coach and author of *The Next Act*

The Wisdom Collection is an impeccable blend of vulnerability and expertise. I was deeply moved by the transformative insights that permeate every single essay. What an extravagantly inspired read!

—Achim Nowak, 4X author and host of the My Fourth Act podcast

Reading *The Wisdom Collection* felt like sitting down with mentors I never knew I needed. James Twyman's urgency to chase inspiration, Julie Ann Cairns'; journey to inner wisdom, and Carl Ficks' powerful lesson in forgiveness - these stories and many others spoke directly to challenges I've faced. This book doesn't just offer wisdom; it creates a profound sense of connection in our increasingly disconnected world.

—Kate Bee, founder of The Sober School and author of *How to Go Alcohol Free*

As someone who has spent years immersed in leadership, business strategy, and personal development, I found *The Wisdom Collection* refreshingly different. It felt like I was sitting beside each author, hearing the real stories behind their decisions, struggles, and growth. These aren't simple theories or polished

frameworks; they're hard-earned insights from people who have actually walked the path. I loved this book!
—**Alison Vidotto, author of** 22 *Leadership Fundamentals*

The Wisdom Collection brings together 19 powerful stories from everyday visionaries who turned their pivotal life experiences into profound insights. In a world of quick fixes and shallow soundbites, this anthology offers something richer—truths learned through adversity, compassion, and courage. Whether you're navigating personal transformation, deepening your relationships, taking a leap in business, or redefining your purpose, these stories will guide, challenge, and inspire you. This isn't just a book; it's an invitation—to reflect, connect, and make choices that align with who you really are.
—**Ellen Johnson, author, and founder of Serendipity Needleworks**

Stories That Transform How
We Live, Connect, and Lead

The *Wisdom* Collection

Ann Sheybani
and other leading voices

SUMMIT PRESS

Disclaimer: The information in this book is provided for educational and informational purposes only. The personal transformation stories, relationship advice, decision-making strategies, leadership principles, and financial guidance reflect the authors' personal experiences and professional opinions. What has worked for the contributors may not be suitable for every individual or situation.

Names, identifying details, and certain scenarios may have been changed to protect the privacy of individuals involved in the stories shared throughout this book.

For personal challenges related to identity, relationships, major life decisions, leadership roles, or financial difficulties, readers are encouraged to seek guidance from qualified professionals. The authors and publisher do not provide psychological, financial, or legal services and assume no responsibility for how this information is applied.

Summit Press Publishers PO Box 1356 Intervale, New Hampshire 03845

First Edition: 2025

ISBN: 979-8-9852063-7-1

For information about special discounts available for bulk purchase, workshops, retreats, and webinars associated with this book, please contact us at author@summitpresspublishers.com.

Table of Contents

Introduction

I n an age of unprecedented connectivity, we find ourselves paradoxically isolated. Our smartphones keep us
tethered to a constant stream of information, yet many
of us feel increasingly disconnected from wisdom—that deeper,
more substantial understanding that gives life meaning and
direction. We scroll through carefully curated highlight reels
on social media while longing for authentic connection. We
consume bite-sized advice promising quick fixes while our
souls hunger for something more nourishing.

This anthology was born from that hunger.

The Wisdom Collection offers an alternative to the culture
of immediacy and superficiality that characterizes so much
of modern life. Within these pages, you'll find no algorith-
mic recommendations, no viral trends, no "hacks" promising
overnight transformation. Instead, you'll discover something
increasingly rare: hard-earned insights from those who have
walked challenging paths and emerged with genuine wisdom
to share.

The contributors to this collection come from diverse
backgrounds—attorneys and entrepreneurs, psychologists and
writers, spiritual seekers and pragmatic business leaders. What

unites them is their willingness to extract meaning from experience, particularly from life's most challenging moments. Many have turned their wounds into wisdom and their struggles into strength. And now, they offer their insights to you—not as prescriptions to follow, but as invitations to reflect.

The Landscape of Modern Disconnection

The social fabric of Western societies, particularly in the United States, has frayed in recent decades. Research consistently shows declining participation in community organizations, religious institutions, and even informal social gatherings. Political polarization has transformed neighbors into adversaries. The COVID-19 pandemic further accelerated these trends, leaving many feeling adrift in an increasingly fragmented world.

The consequences of this disconnection manifest in concerning statistics: rising rates of anxiety and depression, increasing loneliness across all age groups, and a growing sense that we lack the tools to navigate life's complexities with confidence and clarity. Many of us find ourselves asking fundamental questions: Who am I beyond societal expectations? How do I cultivate connections that nurture growth? When should I leap, and when should I plan? What purpose will give my life meaning?

These are not new questions. They have challenged humans throughout history. What has changed is our context for exploring them. Traditional sources of wisdom—intergenerational relationships, spiritual communities, cultural traditions—have become less accessible for many. Meanwhile, we're bombarded with contradictory advice promising simple solutions to complex problems.

The *Wisdom Collection* steps into this gap, offering neither oversimplification nor abstraction, but genuine insight grounded in lived experience.

The Journey Within These Pages

This anthology is organized into five sections, each addressing a vital dimension of human experience:

Personal Transformation & Identity opens our journey with stories of reinvention and self-discovery. You'll discover how one person found freedom from societal expectations around motherhood through a therapist's revolutionary perspective. Another contributor reveals how embracing imperfection became a catalyst for creative progress. A spiritual seeker contemplates the elusive bridge between knowledge and wisdom. These narratives, along with others in this section, illuminate paths toward authentic selfhood in a world that often rewards conformity.

Relationships & Connection explores the wisdom that emerges in the space between ourselves and others. One author recounts learning the liberating power of forgiveness from a Holocaust survivor rabbi. Another examines how our bodies express what our minds suppress. Each contributor in this section offers insights into navigating the complex terrain of human connection with greater compassion and clarity.

Decision-Making & Risk addresses how we navigate uncertainty in both personal and professional realms. Contributors distinguish between calculated risk-taking and recklessness, advocate for immediate action on creative impulses, and challenge the conventional wisdom about making ourselves "irreplaceable." Together, these perspectives offer a nuanced approach to making choices in a world where the path forward is rarely clear.

Authentic Leadership & Purpose invites us to consider how we might contribute meaningfully to the world. You'll learn why businesses built around clear "centering principles" create more meaningful success, why customized approaches that honor individual circumstances matter, and how intellectual property can be reframed as a value driver rather than a cost center. These chapters demonstrate how clarity of values creates both personal fulfillment and professional impact.

Financial Wellbeing & Security concludes our journey by addressing our relationship with money—often one of our most emotionally charged but least examined connections. Authors illuminate the emotional dimensions of financial conversations and offer practical guidance for financial safety during challenging relationship transitions. Both reveal how financial wellbeing requires both tactical knowledge and emotional intelligence.

How to Read This Book

The wisdom contained in these pages isn't meant to be consumed passively. Each chapter serves as both mirror and window—reflecting aspects of your own experience while opening views into perspectives you may never have considered. The authors don't offer simplistic solutions but rather invite you into a deeper relationship with life's essential questions.

Here are four ways you might approach this collection:

Read sequentially. The book's organization creates a natural progression from internal transformation to external application of wisdom. Following this path allows you to build a foundation of self-knowledge before exploring how wisdom manifests in relationships, decisions, leadership, and financial wellbeing.

Begin where you're seeking. If you're navigating a particular challenge, you might start with the section most relevant to your current circumstances. Struggling with a major decision? Turn to Section Three. Reconsidering your professional direction? Section Four might offer valuable perspectives.

Follow the resonance. As you read, certain passages will likely strike a chord—perhaps a sentence that captures something you've always felt but never articulated, or a perspective that challenges your assumptions in a productive way. When you encounter these moments of resonance, pause. Let the insight settle. Consider how it might apply to your own circumstances.

Return and reflect. Wisdom reveals itself gradually, often when we least expect it. You might read a chapter today and appreciate its surface message, only to discover deeper layers of meaning months later when life presents a situation that brings the wisdom into sharper focus. Consider this book a companion on your journey—one worth revisiting as your circumstances and questions evolve.

A Community of Wisdom-Seekers

In creating this anthology, we've brought together diverse voices united by their commitment to authentic transformation. But this community extends beyond the contributors whose words fill these pages. It includes you, the reader, and all those with whom you might share these insights.

In an era of increasing polarization and isolation, there is something revolutionary about creating spaces where wisdom can be shared across differences—where we recognize that growth often happens at the edges of discomfort, and that our most valuable insights frequently emerge from our most challenging experiences.

Whether you're navigating a major life transition, building a values-driven business, or simply seeking more intentional ways of being, these transformative lessons will illuminate your path and empower your journey. More importantly, they remind us that wisdom isn't a destination but a practice—one that flourishes when cultivated in community.

We invite you to receive these stories not as prescriptions but as possibilities. To engage with them not as consumers but as co-creators of meaning. And perhaps, when the moment is right, to contribute your own hard-earned wisdom to this ongoing conversation.

The journey begins with turning the page.

Section 1:
Personal
Transformation &
Identity

This Lifetime

Jennifer Jordan

I was struggling with an anguish that too many women have suffered since the Big Bang created Earth, or at least since female hominids roamed it. And my anguish was only getting worse as I approached my thirty-fifth birthday. That godforsaken biological clock was deafening, birthday after birthday reminding me that my youthful hormones were slipping away, and with them my chances at motherhood.

Dread loomed, and then, on a quiet Tuesday morning, it vanished. Forever.

That Tuesday, I sat in the chair facing Robert. I didn't have a car, so every Tuesday at 7 a.m. I bumped my bike down the front stairs of my apartment building and rode the twenty miles round trip to his office, regardless of the weather, which in Boston often made for a challenging commute. There were times I arrived soaked to the skin by rain, sometimes by sweat.

Other rides left my hands and feet numb with the cold. More than once I had to lift my bike over piles of plowed slush and snow that clogged the streets. The only times I called to cancel were during white-out blizzards, which would have been beyond suicidal to navigate on streets shared with SUVs, delivery trucks, buses, and of course, plows, all swerving and blinded by horizontal snow.

I had been coming to the chair for months, seeking solace as I cried through session after session reliving past wounds and grieving the life I wasn't living, a life that somehow was out of reach but one that I desperately sought.

That particular Tuesday Robert said, "Let's talk about what you are actually grieving. Can you name it?"

I hesitated, wanting my answer to be wise and strong and yet clever and poignant. I wanted him to like me, find me interesting, compelling even, and most of all confident and sure. Why *was* I grieving and how much did I want to reveal?

I had been introduced to Robert at my friends' wedding four years before. He had been their therapist before they finally made it to the altar, and during the ceremony, he gave a beautiful elegy about relationships and their pitfalls, love and its trickery, childhood trauma and its poison. I listened, hearing the words but not processing them through my filter, *my* life. While I was impressed that my friends shared their very personal struggles during their own wedding ceremony, I knew that *I* would never need a pre-marriage therapist, for heaven's sake! I was too smart, too savvy, too independent to choose a relationship that needed therapy *before* it was even official. I was thirty-one years old then and had deftly avoided the train wrecks of boyfriends. Yes, I had had my share of train wreck *dates*, but was always able to cut those disasters short. I was smug in my assuredness, smug in my not needing a boyfriend, and smug that I would eventually find just the right one.

Like many women who came of age in the 1970s, mine was the era in which women gained more power, more autonomy, and yes, more liberation than any previous generation. Many of us had nothing *but* choices and our own money to make them. We had good jobs, even careers. We paid our own rent, bought our own clothes, had our own bank accounts, planned and paid for our own vacations. But most of all, we could choose to marry or not marry, have children or not. And while I wanted to have a family, I didn't overly worry about when, just with whom. I had plenty of time. Discussion of biological clocks hadn't yet become part of the vernacular, mainly because that ticking clock only became heard when so many of my generation didn't have children in our late teens and twenties, as women had done for eons.

Yet even with all of our freedoms, marriage and motherhood were still being promoted as *proper* life goals. Yes, careers were important, society said, but they could never replace children; they could never be as vital, life-affirming, rewarding. How many times had we heard fabulously famous and successful women answer the question "What do you consider your greatest accomplishment?" with "My children." Too many times not to start believing it.

Still, we young women of the 1970s took our freedom for granted, ignorant in our belief that women had always been able to choose their destinies, American women anyway. When I interviewed Erica Jong a decade after she wrote *Fear of Flying*, she rather testily told me that my entire generation "has no appreciation for the sacrifices *we* made so that you could enjoy all of this self-determination." I remember glancing at her knee-high hose, clunky shoes, pilled sweater, and frizzy hair, brittle from over-bleaching, and feeling a measure of pity. *Poor woman*, I thought. *She is just getting old and tired, no longer the sexy author who coined the phrase "the zipless fuck."*

She was right, of course. I and my generation *were* totally arrogant and ignorant of history and assumed we could have it all – happy marriages with supportive husbands, healthy babies, rewarding careers, financial security, and of course, an effortless contentment. Why shouldn't we have it all and more? Our privilege knew no bounds. I had been in my mid-twenties when I interviewed Jong, trusting, *knowing*, I would soon meet my husband, and then get to work with the rest of the list of my entitlements. Then thirty came and went and still no husband or babies in sight. For all of my confidence, I didn't want to be a single mother. I had seen too many miserable ones, alone and exhausted as they wrestled screaming children through airports, mopped up vomit from the grocery store floor, or handed their last quarters to the cashier for a box of Pampers.

No thank you. When I had children, I was going to have backup.

Miraculously, when I was thirty-one, I met my backup, a man I could not only love, but more importantly, live happily with. Then, I waited. Thirty-two, thirty-three, thirty-four – my birthdays relentlessly ground forward while I awaited the ring, maybe even presented with a sweet flourish on his bended knee.

Year after year, I waited through endless, agonizing birthdays, Thanksgivings, Christmases, New Years, and of course fucking Valentine's Day. Goddamn, motherfucking Valentine's Day. Whoever invented it, they were not a single thirty-something woman. But no ring came.

It took me nearly four years to realize the agonizing truth; my backup just didn't love me, not enough anyway. Worse, I saw he wasn't strong enough to admit it. So, just before my thirty-fifth birthday, I was the one who ended it. I limped away, doubled over in pain and loss, fearing that I was walking away from my best, maybe last chance at motherhood as that cruel clock ticked ever louder.

I was still bent and broken months later as I sat sobbing in Robert's chair, searching for a reprieve from the sadness that that was my one chance and that I wouldn't be given another. And I was terrified that that was it, and that the life I was living, as rich as it was hosting my own radio talk show, reporting for NPR and PBS news programs, and writing feature profiles for major magazines, was not enough and never would be.

Robert sat quietly waiting for my sobs to subside. His sharp angular face was calm and closed, revealing nothing. When

I finally blew my nose and straightened up in the chair, he leaned forward.

"I am Buddhist," he began, "so these are my beliefs. You can believe them or not believe them, but know that *I* believe them." He paused and I nodded my understanding.

He continued. "I have listened to your life story for months, heard of your friends and family and the children in your life, and of your devotion to them." He paused again and took a deep breath. "Here's where the Buddhism comes in. In your past lives, you have been a mother hundreds of times. And, in the lives to come, you will be a mother hundreds of more times. Let *this* lifetime be about something else."

Even now, three decades later as I write this story for the first time, tears fill my eyes. Tears of salvation, relief, and redemption. Indeed, it didn't matter that I wasn't a Buddhist, didn't matter that I didn't have the same conviction of past and future lives, didn't even matter if it wasn't true. He believed it as an absolute fact. And his confidence bestowed on me a grace that has remained all these years.

With his words, I was freed of a burden I had carried but been unable to name. I had been led to believe that the pain, anguish, anxiety, fear, and grief were all my fault for not having fulfilled some vital mandate needed to define my life. Now, with Robert's assured edict, I could breathe. Better yet, I could settle into the life I was already living, and celebrate its successes rather than bemoan the one thing it didn't contain.

Let this lifetime be about something else.

And I did. I sublet my apartment, packed my duffels, and followed a story to K2, the second-highest mountain on Earth and one of its deadliest. I was determined to do the hands-on research necessary for what became my first book and documentary. I returned to the mountain two years later, literally stumbled across the skeletal remains of the first man who died on the mountain in 1939, and his story became my second book.

Let this lifetime be about something else.

And it is. K2 not only provided me rich professional fodder, it introduced me to my husband and for the past 25 years we have traveled the world together, working, playing, writing, filming, and always adventuring.

Let this lifetime be about something else.

And while I often wonder what this life would have looked like with children, I no longer mourn my life without them. Because *this* lifetime *is* about something else.

Jennifer Jordan is an award-winning author, filmmaker, and screenwriter with decades of experience as a news anchor and investigative journalist. Her first book, *Savage Summit*, chronicles the lives and deaths of the first female summiteers of K2. Her second book, *Last Man on the Mountain*, examines the 1939 American K2 expedition in which the first person died on the mountain and whose skeletal remains Jordan found at its base. In 2016, she directed and produced *3000 Cups of Tea*, a documentary revealing the flawed *60 Minutes* report on philanthropist Greg Mortenson. In addition to her own books, she has ghostwritten and co-written three others.

To learn more about Jennifer Jordan's award-winning books, films, and writing, visit www.jenniferjordan.net or scan the QR code.

Let it Be Bad

Carla Panciera

T he summer after my father died unexpectedly, I posted my students' final grades and moved home, ostensibly to keep my mother company. I fooled no one, least of all her.

I was twenty-eight years old and woke regularly from disturbing dreams of my father. I wanted my mother nearby.

In every dream, I understood he was dead. I could see the coroner's stitches on his lips, the flesh disintegrating on his hands. In one more innocuous dream, my father explained that heaven was like Costco, a store he had never entered.

"What does that mean?" I asked. "Can you buy tires there? Are you happy?"

"I told you," he said, "if you ask questions, I can't stay."

Early in the mornings, I sat at the table, recounting the previous night's visits to my mom without sparing any details.

"Any plans for today?" she'd ask.

Nothing, though certainly, I was free to at least write. Mostly, I paced around the house, then decided I needed a change of scene. Then, as soon as I arrived elsewhere, I desperately wanted to return to my mother's house.

When the time arrived for me to attend a weeklong Teachers as Writers workshop led by Peter Elbow, I hesitated. I'd signed up months before when I had no idea what that summer would bring.

My mother said, "You need to go."

As a child, when asked what I wanted to be when I grew up, I said, "A writer." It wasn't a profession so much as an identity, a fact as clear to me as my eye color. I wrote on everything from grocery store sales fliers to important documents. In college, I majored in English and earned a graduate degree in poetry before deciding to teach high school, but although I *felt* very much like a writer, I wasn't writing. I started plenty of things but couldn't finish them. Instead, I dedicated myself to learning how to teach my students how to do what had always come naturally to me. Thus, my attendance at the workshop at the University of Massachusetts in Amherst.

In college and in graduate school, workshops focused on the work. Participants might get their feelings hurt, but we learned to separate the work from its writer. Don't take it personally, we reminded ourselves, however ineffective the mantra. These experiences reminded me of slicing open an earthworm in biology to see what it looked like inside. *No offense, creature*, we thought, fascinated that anything existed inside something so previously unknowable. That the specimen lay in ribbons when we had finished moved us not at all.

But I quickly learned that Peter Elbow believed writers focused too much on making mistakes, forcing them to edit thoughts and feelings. A terrible thing. His workshop would be all about thoughts and feelings. We had to emote, express, reveal. *I'm not here for therapy*, I thought angrily. *Nothing to see here.* As people offered up soul-bearing free writes, I found myself longing for the bruising days in *normal* workshops where, okay, you got your soul sucked out of you via your nostrils, but your only job was to sit quietly and take notes. The last thing I wanted to do was to end up confessing to strangers how my Depression-era parents, neither of whom had graduated high school, believed so much in my ridiculous dreams of being a writer that they embraced not only my pursuit of an imprac-tical undergraduate degree but also celebrated my master's in poetry. Then, my dad went and died before I'd done anything with my education or come clean and declared myself a fraud.

Each night, as I returned to my dorm room and switched on the useless fan I'd paid extra for, I stared at my notebook, wondering how any of the touchy-feely stuff in class was sup-posed to help me to write. That was the end goal, to conference with Peter over a draft of either poetry or prose that would be included in our end-of-course anthology. I'd done quite enough feeling that summer, thank you. Now, I just needed to produce something that wouldn't embarrass me.

One morning in this therapy-disguised-as-writing-workshop, Peter and his teaching assistant performed a dramatic reading of a poem from *The Wishing Bone Cycle*, a book of narrative poems by Swampy Cree tribespeople translated by Howard Norman. The poems described a coming-of-age tradition where tribal members are renamed based on personality—names like Rain Straight Down, Eyebrows Made of Crows, or Ties Himself in Knots. Today, we'd call the performance cringey, these workshop leaders echoing one another, repeating lines, changing the timbre of their voices. I squirmed but also marveled at their complete lack of inhibition. Meanwhile, I braced myself for what I knew would follow: our turn. My group and I performed *Who Calls the Mud Places* in as straightforward a way as possible, dividing the poem and reading, with minimal expression, our third of it.

Afterward, Peter asked us to share how we received our own names. Clever trick—using one activity that forces us to expose our vulnerability and then encourages us to open up further.

"My name is a variation of my father's," I said. Next.

One woman said, "I'm named Margaret after my grandmother. Except my grandmother's real name was Mexico."

Margaret described her grandmother's marriage into a wealthy family whose matriarch insisted no daughter-in-law of hers could be called Mexico and renamed her.

The pain of that story felt familiar, though it took me some time to realize the emotion as grief. This is a story about loss, I thought. Finally, the germ for a piece of fiction.

For the next few days, I tried futilely to write a short story about Mexico, then gave up. A poem was out of the question. My dismal experience in the master's program had convinced me I would never be a poet. However, as an undergrad, I had been required to produce one personal essay a week for two semesters. I resorted to that when all else failed (as it frequently did). The next day, I reported for a one-on-one conference with Peter, who asked what I was working on.

I explained how inspired I had been by Margaret's story. "I wanted to write a short story, but I can't. And I can't write a poem. So I'm going to write an essay instead."

Because Peter waited as quietly as any good therapist for me to continue, I expounded on the failed drafts, the dead ends. Finally, he stopped me.

"I hear a lot of can'ts," he said. Unlike other professors, he did not sit at a desk. Instead, he sat on a chair across from me. "What I wonder is, what you're so afraid of?"

Afraid of? The man was out of his mind. But he wouldn't trick me because the thing I most feared had already occurred.

The night before my father's funeral, my best friend sat with me after everyone else had gone to bed.

"You know what the biggest emotion I feel is?" I said.

Teresa said, "Fear."

She was right. What would this feel like? What would happen next?

But here I was—surviving. I was okay.

"Listen," Peter said—I sat up, had my mouth open to call out his bullshit, to flee his office, to tell him to point out flaws in characterization, pacing, the overuse of weak verbs, and stop with this New Age lunacy—except he didn't say *listen* the way some people said it. Instead, he implied that he wanted whatever he was about to say for me, not for him. "Write the story, Carla. Let it be bad."

I'm not going to cry in front of Peter Elbow, I thought.

Let it be bad.

Four words.

No one had ever given me that license, including—especially—me.

Whatever grief would demand of me, the fear that had been with me the longest had been my failure to write. To finish something. To succeed at the only thing I really wanted to do. I'd told everyone I'd ever met that I was a writer. When would I have anything to prove that? Instead, I had done so many other things, easier things at which to excel.

I returned to my room and wrote the story, freewriting, as Peter had taught us, through the roughest patches. *No one has to see it*, I told myself. *Not until you're ready.*

I went home and wrote more stories, poems, essays, and collections of the above.

Every time I get stuck, including as I write this, I hear Peter Elbow. Whenever I pick up a paintbrush to freshen up a room, attempt a new activity, try a new recipe, or change up a lesson plan for my students, I hear Peter Elbow: *Let it be bad.*

"What are you afraid of?" he asked. The most motivational question ever posed to me.

I was afraid then; I am afraid even now, to fail, afraid to look foolish, afraid of not achieving what I set out to achieve. Just like everyone else. But if I am unwilling to risk that, what will I ever have to show for it?

In the midst of those earliest days without my father, I felt acutely the terror of the unknown. I couldn't hide that from Peter Elbow.

My father was a dairy farmer. His life required physical endurance, adherence to a strict schedule, and minimization of risk. I inherited his practicality and pragmatism. I worked beside him and gained confidence in his logical approach to completing the day's tasks.

But my father also loved to sing in Italian as he finished up night milking. He'd climb down from the tractor in the midst of spring plowing to pick me Mayflowers. He could identify every plant that grew around us, bird calls, cloud patterns. He made me aware of the world around me, an essential perspective for a writer.

He taught me that, in the midst of heartbreak and despite the fear of the unknown, beauty persists and inspires. It's worth whatever risk it takes to explore it, to capture it on the page.

Carla Panciera's short story collection, *Bewildered*, received AWP's Grace Paley Award and was published by the University of Massachusetts Press. Her poetry collections include the Cider Press Award winner, *One of the Cimalores*, and the Bordighera Press Award-winning *No Day, No Dusk, No Love.* A third collection is forthcoming. She was the James E. Kilgore Scholar in Nonfiction at the Bread Loaf Writers' Conference and is the recipient of an Individual Artist Grant in Creative Nonfiction from the Massachusetts Cultural Council.

Her newest book is *Barnflower: A Rhode Island Farm Memoir.*

A retired high school English teacher, Carla lives in Rowley, Massachusetts.

Discover Carla Panciera's award-winning short stories, poetry collections, and her Rhode Island farm memoir at carlapanciera.wordpress.com or scan the QR code.

The Snake of Innocence

Julie Ann Cairns

This is a story of striving without arriving. There might be no moral to this story—except to say that if there's any sort of destination, morality alone won't get you there.

I sat near her feet, with legs tucked beneath me, Japanese style.

I'd been guiding people into her arms for a hug for three days. Several hundred of them. They'd lined up for hours, waiting for their turn.

They'd kneel before her, and then, one by one, I'd guide their hands to rest on either side of her chair cushion. She'd pull them into her embrace, holding them gently with her cheek against theirs, and whisper into their ears the words she'd insisted on learning to say in their own language, *"Saiai no musume"* or *"Saiai no musuko"* over and over—Japanese for darling daughter, darling daughter... or darling son, darling son.

I don't remember my first hug much or my second. But the third left a strong impression.

It was in Tokyo, one year prior. I'd flown there from Sapporo—the town where I lived on the north island of Hokkaido—specifically to meet this Indian woman affectionately known as Amma (meaning *mother* in her native tongue of Malayalam).

I'd heard much about this "hugging saint" from a friend whose opinion I valued.

The third time I went up, Amma stopped me before pulling me into her arms. She looked into my eyes with immense compassion. I felt like a river of love was washing through me, pulling me into its current. It took my breath away. No one had ever looked at me like that before. Not that I could remember.

My head began to spin.

Someone helped me find a space on the floor out of the way. I sat down cross-legged, and then I was gone. I don't know how long I sat there, but when I came back to my senses and got up, my legs were stiff.

I know now that the state I spontaneously entered was a deep meditation...but I'd never meditated before, so I had no frame of reference back then.

I was 25 and still in my academic robot era.

Instead of any inconvenient emoting or reflecting—which, whenever I'd allowed it, had always led me into an abyss of depression—I studied and worked.

I'd won a scholarship from the Japanese Ministry of Education to study for an MBA degree at a Japanese university, in Japanese.

Yes, that was a challenging undertaking. Extremely consuming: a side benefit.

I'd also bought an English school, which I ran as a small business.

My days were full, by design: eat breakfast, commute by train for an hour, attend classes at my university, and then spend a couple of hours translating my notes (that I'd scribbled hastily in Japanese) so I could understand them. Commute back again, teach English conversation classes all evening at my school, go home, eat, study until 4 a.m., and then go to sleep. Wake at 11 a.m. and start it all again.

It was a regimented routine, and I performed it as an academic machine.

I was not searching for any deep sense of meaning in my life. There was a certain parchedness inside of me, for sure. And I'd worked hard to get that.

So, I can't tell you why I flew down to meet Amma in Tokyo, but I did, and somehow, it changed me.

On the flight home, I remember thinking, *I wonder what happens to old people who have no one to look after them?* A question, I can assure you, that had never crossed my mind before. Caring much about anyone else's progress through life was not really my style back then. Robots don't do that.

That night, I had a dream. I was being stalked by an enormous snake as I hid under a bridge spanning a vast, deep gorge. It slithered towards me, and rather than run, I let it bite me. I surrendered to the venom and tumbled down into the gorge. As I fell, I felt a comforting sense of relief.

A year later, I was at Amma's feet again, helping others experience her embrace. My friend and I had invited Amma to visit Sapporo, and to our surprise, she'd agreed.

By then, I'd graduated first in my class with an MBA and was contemplating my next steps in life.

Since the snake dream, I'd become more aware that my robotic approach to life was not particularly fulfilling. It worked, but only in the way that it works to hold an inflated beach ball under the surface of the water. You can never take your hands off it. You must keep the tension because the ball ever seeks to rise and break the surface. And holding it down gets exhausting after a while.

My academic achievements, which even I—the perfectionist—could admit were impressive, didn't bring praise from my family, who largely ignored them. They also didn't make me feel worthy of love.

Rather than being proud of all I'd achieved, I felt defeated, tired, and lost.

What would it take for me to feel worthy?

My immature mind assumed it was still about some kind of achievement.

I quickly shifted my focus from academic achievement to spiritual enlightenment as a goal. "Amma," I asked through a translator, "what does it take to become spiritually enlightened?"

She laughed. "Well, it's not easy, daughter, but you can try. You must become completely innocent."

What? Innocent? I thought.

Oh no. I'm screwed!

I didn't feel that innocence was attainable for me. I felt stained by layers of shame.

The thing about shame is that it doesn't follow logic, and that's why robots don't experience it.

Childhood sexual abuse, for example. Though perpetrated by a neighbor, it was still my fault because I must have done something wrong to attract it. Right? Illogical, and yet my shame held it to be true. Being the go-to scapegoat of my family system was also definitely my fault because they told me so. Their opinions would not hold up under any decent scrutiny, yet they were good enough for my shame to swallow whole. And I was Christian. Everyone knows that we Christians carry the collective stain of Original Sin.

Layers. Peering through them, I wondered: *What is spiritual innocence anyway?*

I remembered dimly the joyous innocence of my early childhood. Before the staining began. But I had no idea how to return to that state. And, one could argue, it was more like naivety anyway than transcendent spiritual innocence.

Is there some mysterious bridge that spans the gap between knowledge and wisdom? Could crossing it erase my shame and restore a sort of spiritual innocence that's not naive? And suppose I wanted to cross it, then how? As far as I could tell, it can't be crossed solely powered by morality.

I mean, nearly every religion in the world has some version of the same Golden Rule moral code—a version of: *Do unto others only that which you would have done unto you.*

But even if I demonstrated perfect morality in every deed, would that be enough? Would that constitute a return to innocence?

As my daughter remarked recently when we were discussing the topic: "Well, if you need religious rules or the laws of society to make you do the right thing... then maybe you're not really a good person. Maybe you're just a questionable person on a leash."

Huh.

Yes, darling daughter, I want to let the rules go. I want to peel off the layers of expectation around perfect conduct, perfect thought, and perfect intent. I want to let go of the embarrassment, the shame, and the ideas of would've, could've, should've.

I've done my best.

Since meeting Amma over 30 years ago, I've contemplated and reflected. I've meditated and internally renovated. I've catalyzed catharsis. I've tried to become wise. I've turned my mind to uncovering the expectations I'd put on others that I later deemed unmet and uprooting the expectations I felt I hadn't lived up to myself.

I no longer feel unworthy, so that's good. Really, it's a huge leap forward. But I'm increasingly aware that the tool I've been using to achieve "spiritual enlightenment" isn't fully suited to the task.

My mind can't comprehend the wondrous complexity of humanity and the universe. And maybe that's because it's not the right piece of equipment—like trying to take in the whole sky while only looking through a tiny pinhole.

The game's rigged against the mind. But what about the heart?

At this stage, a dose of carte-blanche forgiveness would feel like a relief—forgiveness that I don't have to measure out or decide who gets it and who doesn't.

Instead of trying to engineer, build, and then traverse the bridge...I wait underneath it.

I wait for the Snake of Innocence to find me in my hiding place and sink its fangs of unlearning into me. I wait for the release as its venom (no, elixir?) reaches my heart, connecting me to something much bigger than myself—something my mind could never hope to comprehend but that my heart may expand to hold.

When the snake comes for me, I hope I don't run. I hope I don't cling to what I think I know. I hope I surrender to it. Because if there exists an unending, unbounded, and unconditional love, then I have it already (I always have, I always will), and so do you. I'm immersed in it. There's nothing to do. There's nothing to forgive.

If you were to ask me now:

How can one bridge the gap between knowledge and wisdom?

I wonder if that's even the right question. I'd answer with more questions, like the beginner I really am:

What if that goal is a distraction that stops you from letting go, my friend? And what if letting go of striving (even spiritual striving) is the key to accessing something truly magnificent?

Julie Ann Cairns is the author of the best-selling Hay House book *The Abundance Code: How to Bust the 7 Money Myths for a Rich Life Now* and the director of the documentary of the same name, *The Abundance Code*, which hundreds of thousands of people have watched since its release. It is now available as a three-part series on Gaia.com. Her greatest passion is helping people see how vital an abundant mindset and a supportive belief system are to achieving success and fulfillment in all areas of life.

Discover how to bust limiting money myths and create a life of abundance through Julie Ann Cairns' best-selling book and documentary at www.theabundancecodebook.com

Forks in the Road:
Finding Choice in Grief

Dr. Haley T. Arias

O n the way to the rural Georgian home where I grew up, you come to a fork in the road. My whole life, we always bore left at that fork. Always. In fact, I don't remember ever taking the road to the right. When I became of driving age, I naturally continued to take the left at the fork on the way home. It's as if my car just knew the way. Until one day, I didn't. I took the road to the right instead. You may think this is where I ran into trouble, but in fact, it was the opposite. I discovered other roads that wound and tied back together, saw cool houses, and explored.

I often reflect on this experience when considering how life presents us with a series of forks in the road, each offering an opportunity to choose. Maybe we don't like the options presented, but there are choices nonetheless. Carl Jung once wrote, "I am what I choose to become." I'll return to this wisdom later. How interesting that we often forget, without noticing, that we have the power to choose. Our car simply drives where it normally does.

Grief's Unexpected Detours

There is no more striking example of life presenting forks in the road than when we are hit with grief. Most people think that grief has five stages that occur in a linear progression. How wonderful and tidy that would be, but sadly, that's not the case. Grief, regardless of its source, tends to come at us like we're in an overcrowded wave pool, desperately trying to escape. You think you're making progress toward land, and BAM! another wave takes you down, right into the person in front of you. Grief does this. You don't just lose sight of where you are, but of who you are.

This is particularly true for teens and young adults, where grief often intersects with their developing sense of self. When I was eleven years old, I lost my brother in a tragic car accident. Suddenly, my life changed. There were profound forks in the road everywhere I turned. At the time, I wasn't aware that's what I was experiencing, but I can see now that this loss shaped who I am today through the decisions I made in the aftermath.

I recognize now that I chose to open up instead of withdrawing. Could this be due to my personality, being the youngest in the family, and loving an audience? Maybe. I'm sure that played a huge role in my ability to share my feelings and experiences with others. But another fork in the road that losing my brother "gave me" was the opportunity to decide whether to question everything and everyone around me or to seek deeper meaning from my relationships. Allowing ourselves to view every fork in the road as an opportunity to choose helps us build resilience, which, by the way, is not inherent to us humans but, when developed over time, helps us cope with pain and grief.

The Illusion of Control

I like to think I was quite a savvy little pre-teen, but truthfully, I was no more aware that I was being given choices than the man in the moon. Looking back, I can see that I desperately wanted to connect and no longer thought of myself as just a child. I was now someone who had gone through a terrible tragedy, and it was up to me to help everyone else who had ever experienced loss too. This is surely why I chose the path of deeper, more fulfilling relationships mentioned above.

Then, cut to age twenty, and my life took another unexpected, jarring turn. Finding that my father had died by suicide one morning felt like someone had taken my American Girl dollhouse and shaken it upside down. Oh yeah, and I was in it. Here's where the forks in the road became very evident. Nothing screams, "You're not in control!" like loss, especially suicide loss.

I have never liked being in the passenger seat. This new feeling of no control didn't work well for me. I railed against it and worked hard to control what I could, going overboard trying to reclaim my agency and process the loss. Be beautiful, stay thin, work out hard, get good grades, become a doctor, find a beautiful man, and have some beautiful kids too! I wrestled with the almighty WHY and got angry. I let that anger fuel my drive to hit goals in my career while keeping everyone at arm's length. It worked and looked great until it didn't.

All along the way, I made the choices I thought I was supposed to make. Like letting my car always veer left at the fork in the road, I never chose to try something different. It wasn't until I underwent fertility treatments and faced their challenges that I realized I was veering left again. I was reverting to old patterns. I was angry, withdrawn, and trying to show the world that everything was perfect when it was far from it. This response felt like home.

I remember asking my doctor as we prepared for another round, "Can we just try something different?! Anything different this time?" And it hit me. Yes, yes, I can. I can choose a different path this time. My attitude doesn't have to be negative. I can be a hopeful, positive person. I don't have to live in fear. I don't have to be mad at every pregnant woman I see. I get to choose.

The Challenge of Conscious Choice

I'd love to tell you that knowing we have a choice and remembering it in a moment of grief happens naturally. But usually, it does not happen at all. So often, we think that we don't have any agency; that life happens, and we're just along for the ride. While that's partially true, it's not the full story. We still have little opportunities everywhere to choose.

A young lady named Katie told me about the time she went to a bar with friends a few weeks after her boyfriend died in a ski accident. She felt brave, as it was her first "normal" outing after his death, and she was back at college on her own again. She was so proud of herself for making it through the majority of the evening and having a fairly good time with no meltdowns in sight. But when she went up to the bar to close her tab, her credit card got declined.

Even as she told me the story, Katie was visibly red, embarrassed, and started to cry. According to her, she repeatedly yelled at the bartender, "Run it again, jerk! It's your machine, not my card!" She didn't use the term "jerk," but something worse. If you're thinking my advice was, "How can you choose differently next time?" it wasn't. It was, "Can you see how you have a choice to either continue to beat yourself up over this or extend a little grace to yourself and know that you were doing the best you could at the time?"

Or I, who chose many times to take the left, working too hard, drinking too much, staying mad, and always trying to prove myself to others instead of allowing myself to just be sad. We won't always get it right. It's not about that. That's a perfectionist mentality that can crush a person experiencing grief and loss.

Finding New Routes

We humans like predictability. That's why, at the fork in the road on the way home, it's not even a choice. We just go home. But when we experience something as profound as a death in the family, a divorce, or a failed business venture, we often default to the methods we know—anything to keep us safe. It's usually not until we're sick and tired of being sick and tired that we make a shift. And even then, we can revert to old patterns.

We start to change that old story by becoming aware that there is always a choice. I can be mad that I grew up without my older brother, consumed with trying to figure out my dad's reasoning for leaving the way he did, and constantly question why God took my babies away from me, OR I can choose to be grateful for all that I do have. It's in gratitude that I ensure I don't miss the moments now by getting caught up in the pain of the past. The goal is not to get it right. It's not to look a certain way during the messiest and most painful parts of life.

The goal is to know, in your heart, that you have a choice and that you're making the best one you can in the moment. And sometimes that comes out as yelling at the bartender.

And sometimes that's taking a deep breath and counting the blessings of today. I've had to reframe my thinking around my losses. There were, ironically, beautiful moments in all of them. We start to heal by recognizing the forks in the road when we can and opting for the route that serves our hearts best. That allows us to become.

Becoming, Not Just Surviving

Jung's complete quote says, "I am not what happened to me; I am what I choose to become." Life's tragedies don't have to define us; they can instead be defining moments where we honor ourselves, our families and loved ones, and our opportunities to choose. Just as I discovered new perspectives by taking the right fork on that familiar road, I can become aware and choose gratitude in the crummiest of memories. Choosing to expect the good, not only the bad. Choosing to help when I see others in pain. We can find unexpected beauty in the paths our grief leads us to explore. We can find beauty in our pain if we choose.

Dr. Haley Arias is an author, coach, chiropractor, and professor of biology who has dedicated her career to helping others navigate life's most challenging transitions. Focusing on grief, Dr. Arias combines science and empathy to support those who feel stuck in the wake of loss. Her programs are known for transforming heavy topics into powerful moments of growth. Blending her academic background with lived experience, Arias guides others with clarity, compassion—and just the right touch of humor.

Visit the link to download her guide, *Healing Ain't Easy: Your Imagination Can Help*, and discover how, even in pain, possibility remains.

Do Your Best and
Leave the Rest

Maria Hampton

I was in my early thirties when I moved to Northern Vermont. I will still tell you to your face that it was a conscious decision I had made to chase a different lifestyle. Still, the hard truth was that my life had fallen apart, and "running away from home" was the only skill set that I really had. One day, after beating myself up for months for being a failure, I decided to stifle my anxiety, pack what I could fit of my life into my 2006 Subaru Forester, and get as far away as I could from what had become untenable in the sunny state of Florida.

When I arrived in Northern Vermont, it seemed like a foreign country after spending a decade in the Deep South. Everything was different, right down to the mentality of the average person I met on the street. No one was in a rush here.

Time slowed down. For someone compulsive about punctuality and a little bit of a control freak, this was a slap in the face. After all, I was raised that if you aren't fifteen minutes early, you're late, and anything less than absolutely perfect is not even worth putting forth.

Being raised by a perfectionist is an understatement. My dad always told us to "do our best," but ultimately, our best had better be better than perfect. It was more of an "if you're not first, you're last" mentality.

After my move, one of my first jobs was working at a big hotel. This is where I met Yoga Joe. He asked me about my story, and I gave him the short version. I explained with a straight face that I had *decided* to make a move to better myself, find a better way of life, trying to hide the truth, which was that I really had no fucking clue what I was doing or where I was headed. Somehow, this stranger pulled my story out of me. By the time we were about to part ways, I'd told him how hard I had always tried for perfection, how insurmountable it seemed, and how anxious it made me feel. He looked me dead in the eyes and said, "All you can do is your best. Leave the rest."

Do your best and leave the rest. That's hilarious, I thought to myself. *Leave the rest for who?* The perfectionist in me could not believe that this hippie had spoken those words, let alone that I was in a space to buy into the idea. "Leave the rest." What a joke. It seems so simple-minded. So trivial. Yet, I have never forgotten his words.

I spent the earlier years of my adult life chasing perfection. Perfection in myself, my career, and my relationships, but somehow, I fell short no matter how hard I tried or how much of myself I lost along the way. I always believed that anything short of perfect, anything short of doing it all, was a failure. "If you're not first, you're last."

What I perceived as failures only mounted as I got older. I felt like I was constantly falling short of my goals, but I didn't really have a clear picture of what the outcome should be. Just that I needed to be better, do better. Each job I left, each relationship that imploded, and each move I made felt like a step in the wrong direction. This had to be because I was not doing enough or because I was doing something (or everything) wrong. I could never be sure what this was, so I continued down the only path I knew, looking for perfection in everything I did.

As I struggled to settle into that more perfect life, because if it were perfect, I would have everything I ever wanted, even though I didn't know precisely what that was, I never forgot Yoga Joe or his silly advice. It was not something I ever saw myself embracing until I realized he was right. He didn't mean not to meet a deadline or to "forget" making dinner for my family. The meaning runs deeper than the simplicity of his words.

"Leaving the rest" doesn't have to mean that you have not done something important on your "to-do" list or short-changed the people in your life. It means that you are smart enough and wise enough to know the difference between the extracurriculars and what you truly need to be successful in the moment. That it's OK to prioritize the things that matter to you at the moment and leave the rest for another day. It's not humanly possible to do it all, be it all. To live otherwise means that, at the end of the day, the only person truly disappointed is you (OK, me), and that doesn't make sense.

Every time you grow, you lose something or someone: a habit, a relationship, or a version of yourself. It's true for all of us. Meaning loss isn't about personal failure, although, let's be real, it can feel that way. Maybe shedding the unnecessary is necessary to grow into the best version of yourself. Maybe these things are worth leaving behind in order to become the best or next version of yourself. Maybe perfection isn't doing it all and being it all but focusing on the little things that truly matter.

It sounds like this epiphany should have put me right, yet as the years went by and I settled into this new life, this latest version of myself, the internal conflict continued. Because how can a perfectionist learn to filter out the noise and only focus on what matters? I'm sorry; everything matters to people like me. It's the little things. Trying to adjust to this mindset has not been easy. Taking Yoga Joe's advice to heart without realizing it, I left the restaurant management field, which I'd been in my entire adult life, and took a job at a spa. (If you knew me, you'd find this choice hilarious because I'm the least relaxed, the least bougie person on the planet.) Turns out, I am a spa person; in fact, I successfully run a multi-million-dollar spa for an international hotel company. Notice my emphasis on the word "successful." In other words, I "failed" at restaurants so I could find what I'm good at.

I left a long-term relationship in which I was heavily invested, and I met my husband, the love of my life. Now, that's a man who really lives the mantra, who is a downright expert at enjoying the little things in life.

I regularly get lost in thought, breaking down my workday, wondering what I forgot to do and where I missed perfection by a country mile. It's not unusual for my husband to interrupt that train of thought by pointing out how many birds are at the feeder or the family of deer in the yard. My knee-jerk reaction is to scoff at such simplicity and to stress harder because, God, who doesn't love controlling *all* the hidden variables and assuming absolute power? But then I force myself to remember. I did my best today, and now I am home. Leave the rest. It will either be there tomorrow, or it was not important in the first place. What is important is here. Now.

"Do your best and leave the rest." The rest is just noise.

It turns out that if you release control and let go of your anxieties, you can focus more on the tasks at hand. You can let others be who they are and think what they think so you can do the same. You can truly learn from your setbacks and failures because you do have a part in that game, and it helps to know what that part really is. Amazingly, this leads to faster and more seamless growth. Walt Whitman said, "Keep your face towards the sunshine, and shadows will fall behind you." Perfection: Easier said than done, Dad, but thanks.

Maria Hampton has been a hospitality professional for nearly three decades, focusing on leadership and cultural training. She has held positions in all areas of the hospitality field, from restaurant management to hotels and spas. For the last ten years, she has been a spa leader for Destination Hotels, which is now a Hyatt property. As a student of life, Maria enjoys traveling the world and exploring with her husband.

The opportunity to contribute to this book appealed to her as a way to share some of her life experiences in a fun and different way. She has never seen herself as an author.

They currently reside in northern Vermont with their cat, who is not named after cheese.

Take Control of
Your Thoughts to
Take Charge of Your Life

Susan Axelrod

I mean, you may be clear, focused, and meticulously managing your mind, living your purpose, and ensuring your legacy. For most of us, however, that's an unrealistic claim. We struggle with low confidence, minimal output, unfulfilled desires fueled by social media, information overload, distractions, and difficulty accessing critical thinking. We are products of an over-connected, over-digitized culture.

What's a human to do?

Start by asking yourself, "Am I OK with myself as I am, with my life as it is? Or is there something more that I want?" Perhaps to feel more in charge? Less distracted and mentally hazy? If you are uncertain about feeling in charge of yourself, your life, and your legacy, there is a formula you can learn to create a different way of being.

If you want to change, here's a formula I developed based on centuries of human experience:

**Thoughts are things + You can control things =
You can control your thoughts.**

What does "Thoughts are things" mean? It means that thoughts are tangible entities with real impact—they influence your emotions, behaviors, and ultimately, your outcomes. They aren't just fleeting ideas but concrete elements you can work with.

Too simple, you say? I thought so too until it transformed my life.

For decades, I lived in a state of unwellness fueled by over-achievement. There's nothing wrong with wanting to get it right, but striving for perfection every single time can lead to anxiety if things don't go well. While worrying about every potential future problem, exacerbated by the internet, I clung to past regrets. The result? Overwhelming depression and a breakdown that left me bedridden for ten days. Therapy and medication helped, but only to stabilize me. I had to break through a mindset of habituated negative perseveration.

Through a deliberate self-help journey—a series of mindful transitions—I learned that thoughts are things and that I could control them. I began by asking myself a few questions: "What if I don't take control of my thoughts? What if I continue down this path of anxiety and depression? Where will it lead?" The answers jolted me out of the apathy of negative ruminations that were draining my quality of life. Thoughts that had run roughshod over me, triggering anger and co-opting my inner peace and self-esteem. I started controlling my thoughts with surprising results. Certainty and confidence found me.

Twenty-five years ago, I discovered the basis of the Mindset Transformation Formula during a long commute. I listened to inspirational speakers and philosophers. I remember looking at my CD player and talking to myself in the car: "So, wait. Thoughts are things? Things I can control? Do you mean I can control my thoughts instead of letting them control me? Hold on, I need to process this."

I felt so unsettled then (happiness felt elusive) that I decided to "just try it." Imagining that thoughts were things I could control seemed manageable. What was the worst that could happen?

I listened to more speakers discussing "how to achieve what you want," individuals who appeared to have attained what I desired. They were successful in business, published authors, and motivational figures encouraging us to learn mindset transformation, energetic attraction, and intentional manifestation. I transitioned from skepticism to exploration; from there, I sensed the real possibility of relief from my troubled mind. I created my first Transformation Tip: "Change the words 'have to' to 'want to,' transitioning from resistance to flow." I wrote it, thought it, practiced it, and eventually, I began to see things differently. "Having to" do something felt outside my control. Mindfully wanting something put me confidently in charge. I found my footing and learned about emotional regulation and positivity. I discovered mindfulness tools to balance my nervous system.

Oh, but don't misunderstand, I now understand why mindfulness is called a 'practice.' I have been practicing for decades. We are burdened humans, facing endless opportunities to overcome obstacles through mindful living and conscious choices.

The Formula in Action

I learned this from one of my first coaching clients. During our discovery call, this smart, talented, and passionate man shared his "wildest imagination," his deepest desire. He had an existing Facebook group but wanted a global movement with meetups, memberships, and meaningful outcomes.

Here's how we applied the formula: I challenged his limiting beliefs and offered a new perspective. I invited him onto a consciousness bridge, and together, we created new thoughts about possibility and legacy. He transformed from "I wish" to "What if" to "Why not me/now?" to "How could?" to "What next?" to "Wow." In this experiential progression, he learned to control his thoughts. Today, he is recognized globally as a confident thought leader. He realized that his self-doubting thoughts shaped his narrative and experiences. He changed his thoughts by asking himself questions, the answers to which were within his control, altering his perspective.

The Process: How to Control Your Thoughts

Here's the process:

1. Figure out the thought you want to think, but keep it simple. A common pitfall is aiming for grand thoughts that feel unachievable. Remember, my first thought was, "Just try it; it can't hurt." It wasn't: "I can achieve ALL of this right NOW" (my Type A anthem).

2. Tune in to your current thought patterns. Notice the thoughts that frequently arise. Are they anxiety-inducing, leading to overwhelm? "I should have, could have, wish I had…" – a negative mindset, feeling behind, unworthy, or unconfident.

3. Create intentional thoughts. Remember, thoughts are things, and you can control them. While creating positive thoughts may be challenging, trial and error can lead to cognitive restructuring. Intentional positive thoughts will help replace negative patterns.

4. Select a visual reminder for the thought you want to reinforce. I learned this tool from someone along my journey: "Every time you see your visual reminder, you will think of your intentional thought." The visual

connects to the thought, boosting confidence. I've used this tool successfully for nearly three decades with every client.

5. Take small actions to move you to the next step (not the entire endgame). As you progress incrementally, you will find the journey becomes more tangible, deepening your commitment to the path.

Does it work every time? Well, yes, it does. If you know the formula and can articulate the thoughts you want to cultivate. However, many create obstacles to their success with thoughts like, "I just can't," "That seems too simple," or "I can't clear my mind." You can overcome these obstacles by asking yourself challenging questions.

Life is complex these days, and it may seem unrealistic to think you can simply control your thoughts. One client hired me to help her organize a move, and she continued working with me for years, stating, "I never imagined that positive outcomes could stem from positive thoughts. I've been a negative person my whole life. Finally, I decided to try it. Gaining control of my thoughts has liberated me."

From Thought Control to Confidence

So, how does it feel to be in control of your thoughts? After feeling like a tumbleweed drifting across time for years, knowing

I could choose my thoughts helped me reclaim my power. I've witnessed how it has helped others do the same.

Mindset transformation is urgently needed today to protect and uplift our struggling society. Critical thinking, focus, decision-making, personal confidence, and strong self-esteem are being surrendered to digital addiction; the internet overwhelms, and an artificial intelligence that provides all the answers, all of which fosters negative rumination. We are losing the art of intuitive experience, and consciousness is fading. But thoughts are things; you can control things!

One final example: I had a client who was the mother of a severely disabled child. She suffered from worry, fear, and emotional abuse from her ex-partner. I encouraged her to confront her negative thoughts and shift her narrative to focus on the strength of her daughter and her own powerful self. It wasn't easy. She worked tirelessly and said she felt "unshackled."

The formula is simple yet profound: Thoughts are things + You can control things = You can control your thoughts. By mastering this formula, you can shift from negative thoughts to positivity, from mental fog to clarity, from anxiety to confidence, and from feeling adrift to taking charge of your life.

Coach **Susan L. Axelrod**, *Confidence Personified* (look her up). Take this quiz to see if *your* mindset is holding you back. (QR code)

Section 2:
Relationships &
Connection

Live to Forgive

Carl R. Ficks, Jr.

———

"**H**e needs our forgiveness, and he needs our love," the rabbi told me as we drove to court. Forgiveness and love are seemingly paradoxical attributes not commonly found in trial lawyers like me. There simply wasn't room for either in the world I occupied in 2006, one I had lived in since 1988. As a lawyer, I was bound by specific ethical rules, including one commanding us to act "with zeal in advocacy upon the client's behalf." Lawyers, including me, have taken "zeal" to unprecedented levels of bravado, obstinacy, and vengeance. Forgiver and lover? Forget about it.

Yet, without forgiveness and love, you run the risk of ending up with a toxic and harmful mix of anger and resentment.

Nelson Mandela said, "Resentment is like drinking poison and then hoping it will kill your enemies." Resentment necessarily means holding onto anger, and that's decidedly unhealthy. "Studies show there may be a link between patients with increased anger and a higher risk of developing premature coronary heart disease and suffering coronary events," says Druenell Linton, M.D., a Piedmont Healthcare cardiologist.

Mandela and medical studies be damned. I wasn't in the mood to forgive or spread love when I headed to federal court in New Haven, CT, to support one of my wife's brothers, a guy ensnared in a wide-ranging corruption scandal involving Connecticut's governor. Judgment day had arrived. Having pled guilty before trial, Bill was to be sentenced for his misdeeds.

Their grandfather, an Italian immigrant, founded a construction company in 1923. With the help of his sons, the company grew and became one of the most recognizable names in the industry. More than 100 years later, it is part of CRH, a global Fortune 500 company.

Carol's brother appeared to have it all, or at least everything I thought I needed but never had when I was young. Money. Cars. Vacations. Travel. A built-in career in the family business. The scandal dominated the Connecticut news cycle from when the federal investigation exploded in the press in 2002 through his 2005 guilty plea and onward to the 2006 sentencing. Print and broadcast media relentlessly pursued him with special vitriol, sparing no one. While the press marauded through his life, his family's honor, prestige, and sterling reputation became collateral damage. I had a front-row seat to a living prodigal son, no different than the one portrayed in Luke's gospel. The one who had it all and then squandered it. How could he have done such a thing?

There was simply no escaping this public circus. When the indictment dropped in 2004, Carol and I were in Puerto Rico celebrating our tenth wedding anniversary. I learned of the indictment while watching CNN on a hotel treadmill, thinking, *This is a hell of a way to crash our party.* Bill would plead guilty on my birthday in 2005. My first thought was, *Why won't this guy leave us alone?* My second thought was, *Good.*

Although willing to attend his sentencing in a show of familial solidarity (really, to support my wife), at that time, I had committed to never forgiving him for the collateral and very material damage his conduct wrought upon my wife and her family. I've been an endurance athlete most of my adult life, so when I commit to something, I am committed. Very little, if anything, will move me away from the end goal.

Despite my own simmering and molten emotions about the situation in which he found himself, I asked Bill how I could support him on that fateful sentencing day. "Please give the rabbi a ride to court," he asked. So that's what I did.

The "rabbi" was 91-year-old Henry Okolica, known to most in Connecticut as "Everyone's Rabbi." As a young man, Rabbi Okolica survived the Nazi persecution campaign Kristallnacht, or "Night of Broken Glass," a campaign of deadly tyranny against Jews in 1938. Later imprisoned by the Nazis, he was freed after his wife's family bribed his jailers.

As recorded by the Immigrant Heritage Hall of Fame, Rabbi Okolica often said, "God took care of me...I didn't escape Germany to live my own life. I escaped because God commanded me to be his helper." During the posthumous induction ceremony, his son Daniel said, "It did not make any difference to him who anyone was...To my father, you were simply a human being—and all that mattered to him was helping humanity." An official with Connecticut's Department of Veterans Affairs, at whose hospital the rabbi ministered, once said that he "reaches in and wraps his hand around your heart."

I had spent my legal life nailing hearts to the wall.

My wife and I were, beyond a shadow of a doubt, in the presence of greatness during that ride to court. Not greatness like the sports figures and Hollywood glitterati so revered in today's society, but rather human greatness. Think of Martin Luther King, Mahatma Gandhi, Desmond Tutu, and Oskar Schindler. That kind of greatness.

We chatted amiably as the diminutive rabbi, who, while sitting in the front seat of my car, could barely see over the front dashboard. He provided a gripping recollection of the Night of Broken Glass, transporting me to November 1938 and effortlessly dropping me into the middle of days of mayhem, death, and destruction. He told me that it should have been called the "Night of Insanity" because the Nazis didn't just break glass; they "broke the heart of civilization." The rabbi wove together how this humanitarian crisis indelibly shaped and drove his life as God's helper. Ever the teacher, he said, "When people think that other human beings are less than they are, then they really are nothing themselves." He told me that we should "bear no malice and seek no vengeance" and to not "cast away God's precious gift of love and kindness."

Rabbi Okolica then pivoted and, sensing my transparent contempt for the reason underpinning our drive to court, took me by the metaphorical hand and helped me understand what my brother-in-law needed at the deepest level possible. Not only what he needed that morning but also in the dark days looming on the horizon, days that would undoubtedly be spent in a federal prison camp.

"He needs our forgiveness, and he needs our love," said the rabbi.

Did I think Bill was less than me because of his guilty plea? Had malice permeated my inner core, thus driving me to seek vengeance by committing to never forgiving him for squandering all that he had? If the rabbi could find forgiveness for the terror unleashed upon him in 1938 and not cast away God's precious gift of love, then so could I.

By the time I walked into court in New Haven one hour later, I had completely reversed course. My vengeful desire to watch, in real time, the prodigal son's punishment evaporated. My heart ached for the public humiliation he and his family were about to endure and for the ensuing lawful seizure of Bill's liberty. I had forgiven him, courtesy of God's helper,

Rabbi Okolica, who reached in and wrapped his hands around my heart.

During the lengthy and tumultuous sentencing proceeding, Bill apologized, took full responsibility, and offered no excuses for his conduct. He said he would "spend the rest of [his] life trying to make up for...the damage caused." Before I picked up the rabbi that morning, a cynical me would have categorically rejected this mea culpa as privileged window dressing. The transformative journey, however, allowed me to accept and believe what Bill said.

After the judge handed down a 30-month prison sentence, he commanded my brother-in-law into the custody of the United States Bureau of Prisons. No reality television show could touch what unfolded that morning.

Bill would go on to serve his time in a minimum-security federal prison camp in Otisville, NY, 120 miles from my house in Connecticut. The ripples from the gift that Rabbi Okolica gave me were profound. My wife and I, along with our two daughters, would regularly visit Bill on Saturdays. In the fall of 2006, I ran a Sunday morning marathon in Scranton, PA. Knowing that the drive to and from Scranton would bring us through the outskirts of Otisville, I told my wife that on our drive home, I'd like to stop at the prison. No Sunday visits were allowed except with counsel, and that's the hand I played. Despite my fatigue from having just run 26.2 miles, I knew it was important to visit Bill. To let him know that he had not been forgotten. To let him know that he was loved.

I frequently wrote letters to Bill and sent him paperback books to read, anything to keep his mind off the monotonous boredom of the prison camp. I also became a fierce defender, most notably when people would comment that 30 months in a minimum-security prison was "nothing." I'd ask them to tell me the precise moment they'd ever had their liberty taken away. When my question was inevitably met with dulled, expressionless silence, I would dismissively tell them they could likely not even handle a four-hour airport flight delay without climbing the walls.

Bill's journey also provided a teachable moment for our daughters. My wife and I discussed what to tell the girls, and we decided it was easy—we tell them there are rules in life, Uncle Bill broke them, and he's making up for it. To this day, he has a close and warm relationship with my daughters, and I trace it back to the prison visits. That would never have happened if I had held onto the resentment, anger, and bitterness I felt before my car ride with God's helper.

Rabbi Okolica taught me not to drink the poison and to live to forgive, and it made me a stronger person. I often wonder how many more people he helped during his 103 years on this earth.

Carl R. Ficks, Jr., J.D., helps leaders fire up their teams, boost engagement, solve problems collaboratively, and lead with emotional intelligence. A former trial lawyer with over 30 years in the trenches, Carl knows how to thrive under pressure—and teaches others to do the same. He is a trusted advisor to organizations and nonprofits, an endurance athlete who believes resilience is a superpower, and a frequent voice on leadership and legal podcasts. Carl is also a contributing author to *The Difference: Essays on Loss, Courage, and Personal Transformation.*

To get in touch with Carl or enquire about his services, scan the QR code or go to https://carlficks.com/

The Body Will Find a Way to Express What the Mind Suppresses

Regina Graziani

My body was once merely a tool I wielded—tired, sick, injured—it didn't matter. My days were packed with court deadlines, university program responsibilities, and parenting obligations. As a seasoned attorney and educator, I thrived in high-stakes environments that rewarded intellect, endurance, and relentless productivity. I kept pushing through no matter the cost.

I told myself I was "fine."

Tired? Yes. In pain? Yes. But I was fine.

Then my body said no. It had whispered for years. Now it roared.

A few years earlier, I was in a car accident that left no visible injuries but rewired everything inside. The traumatic brain injury was subtle and, from the outside, easily overlooked.

Inside, however, everything had changed. My vision was blurred. Light felt like daggers. Migraines hit suddenly, stopping me in my tracks. Words became elusive or vanished mid-sentence. Knowledge—court rules, lectures I'd presented for years—disappeared. I didn't know this person. I felt ashamed. And furious.

And because I looked fine, I presumed I should be fine.

I worked hard to return to the person I was before the accident: doctors, specialists, bodyworkers. Rest that never restored me. Mental processing that never sped up. Gut protocols that left me violently ill. Injuries that refused to heal, despite countless rehabilitation efforts.

So, I worked harder. If my body were in better shape, if I could run faster, lift heavier, and push through the pain, I thought it would return me to the person I used to be. I desperately wanted the mind-body connection I once had to return; everything would fall into place. I would return to being the happy, successful, strong person I once was.

I didn't.

My nervous system stayed stuck in high alert. Every workout became another wound.

So, I leaned on what I knew: work, structure, achievement.

It was safe. Predictable. I could do my job with one hand tied behind my back, and some days, it felt like I was. But even as I excelled, I felt it: the misfit. My roles didn't fit. My life didn't fit. I kept waiting for something to click, to shift, to go back to "normal." It didn't.

No title, no treatment, no accomplishment could override what my body already knew:

I was living out of alignment. And it was done whispering.

The warning signs continued to accumulate. Physical injuries, disturbed sleep, digestive issues—each dismissed, individually, as insignificant. Until one day, my back seized up so entirely that I collapsed. My body had finally done what my mind refused to: it forced me to stop.

Sprawled on the floor, immobilized by pain, I understood a profound truth: my body wasn't failing me—it was protecting me. This wasn't a betrayal but an act of desperate self-preservation.

Reading Gabor Maté's *When the Body Says No* was an "aha" moment. Maté articulated what I had been experiencing but couldn't express: "You are not your results. You are the context in which your results happen."

What we in the legal profession rarely discuss is how our training actively disconnects us from our bodies. We're taught to prioritize rationality over instinct, precedent over intuition, and the standards of a "reasonable person" over our own internal guidance systems. This professional conditioning doesn't just shape how we practice law—it transforms how we inhabit our physical selves.

High-achieving professionals are particularly vulnerable. Our culture rewards intellect and logic, especially in the legal profession where reason reigns.

The professional paradox is this: the very qualities that make us successful—analytical thinking, emotional detachment, relentless work ethic—are precisely what disconnect us from our bodies' wisdom. We're rewarded for transcending physical limitations, not honoring them.

To other high-performing professionals hearing the whispers—or feeling the roar, know this:

Your body knows who you are.

And it will do everything it can to lead you back home.

The Dangerous Myth of "Fine"

"I'm fine."

It's the most socially acceptable lie we tell—and most likely to cost us our well-being.

I lived in a constant state of low-grade anxiety, fueled by performance and responsibility, believing that was the price of success. That this relentless pace, this internal tension, was normal. Every successful attorney I knew lived like this.

High-performance cultures treat "fine" as a requirement—particularly in demanding fields like law, academia, and parenting. Admitting "I'm not fine" is impossible.

My back injury wasn't random. It was the culmination of years of ignoring the whispers after my auto accident—years of believing that working hard, pushing hard, were normal.

"Fine" is not a destination; it's a numbing limbo between truth and collapse.

Your Body's Inescapable Ledger

The body's communication operates on an escalating scale of urgency. First come the subtle messages—tension headaches, disrupted sleep patterns, digestive disturbances. These are the yellow lights many professionals routinely run through. When ignored, the body escalates to more disruptive symptoms— chronic pain, anxiety attacks, recurring illness.

In the legal profession, this escalation plays out against a backdrop of perfectionism. The same attention to detail that makes us excellent advocates makes us terrible at recognizing our limits.

To be clear, these aren't separate warnings. They are our body's red flags indicating we are misaligned with our true selves.

The Revolutionary Act of Embodied Listening

The best advice I ever received wasn't about how to work harder or be more productive. It was this: *Your body is not an obstacle to overcome. It is your greatest ally. Listen to it. Trust it. Respect it.*

I was performing my life rather than living it.

Now, when I speak to other legal professionals, I offer this uncomfortable truth: what we call resilience in our profession is often just sophisticated denial.

Here's the truth high performers don't want to hear: *You can't outwork misalignment.* No amount of success will make up for a life that disconnects you from your body and soul. That's not strength. That's sacrifice. And it's not sustainable.

What emerges when we align with our bodies is something far more valuable than uninterrupted productivity. It's discernment—the ability to distinguish between necessary discomfort and harmful strain, between worthy challenges and self-destruction disguised as ambition.

I noticed when my:

- Breath slowed under stress.
- Jaw clenched when I pushed through stress.
- Stomach dropped at every reluctant "yes."

These physical responses constitute a sophisticated feedback system far more reliable than any performance metric. They are your body's real-time assessment of whether your choices align with your deeper needs and values—information no client evaluation or partner review can provide.

Steve Hardison says, "You are not your results. You are the context in which your results happen." Shifting my context—from performance and perfectionism to alignment—created change.

The Wisdom of Breakdown

My back injury was the alarm I couldn't snooze. But I am grateful for the lesson it taught me: The body is always speaking. It is never betraying you—it's only ever trying to protect you.

We live in a world that rewards burnout and martyrdom. We mistake depletion for dedication. We glorify burnout and call it success. But if success comes at the cost of your health, your joy, your peace—is it success?

What I've discovered is this: true ambition isn't the relentless pursuit of external achievement at all costs. Real ambition is the courage to create a life where your deepest values, including your well-being, are honored. Where success is measured not just by what you accomplish, but by how aligned you feel while accomplishing it.

Don't wait until the roar. Listen now.

When your body says no, it's not the enemy. It's the messenger.

If the roar has knocked you to the ground, take heart. This moment, painful as it is, is your turning point.

It's time to start listening.

Reclaiming Your Body's Wisdom: A Practice

What whispers have you been ignoring? Where have you been pushing past exhaustion, stress, or discontent?

What would it look like if you listened to your body as the wise advisor it is?

What small change can you make today to reconnect with your body and listen to its wisdom?

The path forward isn't about grand gestures or dramatic life overhauls. It begins with these simple practices:

1. **Tune in.** Don't dismiss the whispers—listen deeply, without judgment.

2. **Challenge the dangerous myth of "fine."** Fine is the mask exhaustion wears. Call it what it is.

3. **Redefine strength.** Real strength isn't endurance—it's alignment.

4. **Document your physical responses.** Keep a body journal noting what physical sensations arise during different professional scenarios. What clients, cases, or responsibilities trigger physical tension? What brings ease?

Your body holds the map. Trust it. Take the first step.

In a professional world that values your output over your well-being, listening to your body becomes not just a personal practice but a radical act of resistance. It's declaring that your humanity matters more than your productivity. That your presence—fully embodied, fully alive—is your greatest contribution. Not just to your work, but to a world desperate for models of authentic success.

Regina Graziani, Esq., is a seasoned attorney, academic leader, and public speaker known for her commitment to developing legal professionals. She has over two decades of legal and educational experience. She directs a nationally recognized, ABA-approved paralegal studies program and has taught undergraduate and doctoral law courses. She has handled a variety of complex litigation matters and regularly speaks at legal conferences, professional organizations, and bar associations.

You can connect with her on LinkedIn by scanning the QR code.

Ask for What You Want with Open Palms

Jennifer Lytle

Picture this: You hold your hands out, palms up, vulnerable yet confident. You make a request without demanding a specific outcome. This physical and emotional posture captures the essence of what I call the Open Palms Ask.

The Open Palms Ask is a form of communication that is not attached to a specified outcome. It embodies a posture of vulnerability and authenticity, allowing you to convey your needs, preferences, and desires openly. This approach signifies your willingness to express what you want, feel, prefer, and need. It is a face-forward, shoulders-back stance that remains sensitive to the wants, feelings, preferences, and needs of those with whom you are connected. The Open Palms Ask embraces a both/and perspective, accommodating more than one party's narrow expectations.

This type of ask can be perceived as both an invitation and a query. Unlike a traditional invitation, the Open Palms Ask is not a tool wielded against others; it is not a tactic to pursue a solitary agenda. It does not minimize your needs, reflect false humility, or involve entirely sacrificial concessions.

Why Communication Style Matters

Communication is a skill that exists along a continuum. The Open Palms Ask represents a step on this continuum. Asking for what you want is a foundational entry point into communication at this level. Communication is never a solo event; it requires reciprocity. Otherwise, it becomes a monologue or mere self-talk. Advanced communicators may recognize an indirect ask and respond well to a direct one, but such nuances may be beyond the scope of this chapter. It is essential to acknowledge that communication requires multiple perspectives; connection cannot be overlooked.

The Power of Connection

Substantive relationships are crucial for developing the art of asking. This is cultivated during childhood and continues through parenting within a broader community, but it is just one form of relationship. Connection is paramount.

Attachment has far-reaching effects on life, which is why parenting experts agree that relationships are *the* most significant takeaway from childhood. Material possessions like cars and cash are fleeting, but connection transcends, without negating, the requests made in various relationships. This is encouraging news for those who experienced less-than-ideal attachments in childhood. Healthy attachment can be nurtured in relationships such as therapeutic ones or within a supportive marriage. One client noted that their relationship with their boss helped to mend some of their trust issues.

How Connection Appears in Therapeutic Relationships

The significance of connection in relationships is evident in clinical settings, illustrated by how a client engages with therapy and their counselor. I typically conclude initial evaluations (a fancy term for the first therapy session) with a discussion of two paths in therapy (at least in my practice). The first route is traditional psychotherapy, which allows for exploratory, client-directed "rabbit holes." To engage fully, the client must be willing to embark on a patient journey without the interference of a demanding inner critic pushing for specific outcomes. In short, this approach requires time.

Some of the most profound insights emerge for well-matched clients who are willing to engage in exploratory psychotherapy. This method aligns with the Open Palms Ask, inviting the therapist to join the client's journey. Implicit trust encourages clients to commit to ongoing work, even when immediate results are not apparent.

Conversely, some clients focus explicitly on achieving clinical outcomes from their investment. I have "graduated" (the term "terminated" was poorly chosen) numerous short-term, goal-oriented clients. This primarily linear path involves assessments, evaluations, and re-evaluations as standard components of the process aimed at steering toward the objective. Emotional processing is often overlooked in favor of mastering emotional regulation, assuming it aligns with an identified therapeutic goal. These clients operate from the point on the communication continuum labeled "ask for what you want."

Peter's Open Palms Ask

Peter struggled with uncontrolled anxiety that created challenges in parenting. During our sessions, he eventually shared details about his marriage. He perceived Paola as critical and described behaviors that reflected a lack of emotional regulation. He was always careful in his explanations, demonstrating his commitment to his family and his desire to enjoy family life. He simply didn't know how. Paola needed Peter to support her transformation through maturation, as she had just begun individual therapy. Once he recognized that she required a psychologically safe and emotionally stable partner to uphold his boundaries and personal regulation, Peter was ready. His assignment was to be okay with himself, even if Paola was not. He initiated the development of the Open Palms Ask, aiming to be open and vulnerable about his needs and limitations while granting space for Paola's needs and limitations. Peter was willing to set aside some immediate needs, like gaining respect from his wife, and discovered he had a voice regarding his most pressing concerns. For instance, he committed to speaking up if Paola belittled him in front of their children. He concluded therapy feeling content with his insights as a new starting point in their relationship.

Ask for What You Want, Angie

Another family struggled with connection and communication. Angie wanted me to work with her teenage daughter. We first met for a one-on-one session, during which she referred to a typed list on her phone. I wondered how often she referenced this list when addressing Melanie. According to the list, Melanie was disrespectful, frequently lied about trivial matters, and exhibited moodiness. Angie wanted me to discipline her daughter, presenting a fervent ask for what you want moment. It felt as if she were giving me marching orders, firmly gripping her version of the truth, using it as reins with Melanie... and as whips with me. The priority was correcting behavior, not fostering connection.

Barriers to the Open Palms Ask

We often struggle to employ the Open Palms Ask because facing disappointment, relinquishing perceived control, or sidestepping immediate (even temporary) victories can be difficult. Angie found it challenging to embrace the Open Palms Ask due to her limiting belief that she had done everything right.

Vulnerability can be perceived as an insecure stance; it opens you up to the possibility of not being met, understood, or considered. The Open Palms Ask becomes accessible with a general trust that your needs will be fulfilled. Without this inner assurance that you will be okay no matter what, it can be nearly impossible to lean fully into vulnerability.

A Personal Story: Connection Over Control

After summer camp last year, our daughter Verity wanted to attend the group's ongoing youth nights. Continuing her connections with new friends made sense. While we initially agreed, my husband and I ultimately decided against it. Our reasons had nothing to do with Verity or her friends; the simplest explanation we conveyed was that a geographically closer group would also allow her brothers to participate. We signed her up for the new youth group. Five months after our "no," she still had tears to shed.

Our parenting diligence fostered a deep connection with Verity. Although she was deeply disappointed, shutting us out was never a solution for her.

While driving together, Verity and I passed four churches within a few minutes. She wondered aloud, "Why are there so many churches?" I sighed a deep, pitiful exhale.

"What's wrong with churches?!"

I assumed the matter was beyond her twelve-year-old heart to grapple with, so I lightly shifted the topic. I reminisced about the church I attended during college and the worship leader's ability to draw the congregation into the presence of God.

She shared how that experience mirrored her time at the previous youth group. Verity elaborated on how the messages she heard were rich with meaning, engaging her with the variety of speakers. Often, they would break into small group discussions, which were her absolute favorite. Resistance was futile; her father and I rearranged our schedules and committed to sending her farther north so she could continue to engage with what she found meaningful.

We hadn't changed our minds simply because she asked for what she wanted. She communicated, opened herself to connection, and we reconsidered our position. It wasn't her request that broke the barrier from desire to fulfillment; it was her heart. Had she not talked to me for the sake of connecting, nothing would have changed for her.

The Benefits of This Approach

Why would I be willing to open myself up to the pain of disappointment or the possibility of being denied? The Open Palms Ask feels fundamentally different within us. In contrast, demands, nagging, or manipulation require significant negative thought, time, and personal effort. Do you remember the face-forward, shoulders-back imagery? How does that feel in your body? Take two minutes now. Straighten your back and neck. Open your posture to draw your shoulders back. Expand your chest and use your diaphragm to take a deep breath. The Open Palms Ask feels good when we practice it.

Practical Examples You Can Use Today:

1. At work: "I noticed the coffee pot is empty when I arrive at 8. Can you make a fresh pot if you get the last cup?"

2. At home: "I noticed we've eaten out four times this week. Can we sit down together this week? You choose the day, and we can meal plan. I'd like to meal prep together."

Conclusion: The Heart of Connection

In life, you may get some of what you want some, if not most, of the time. Life offers reasonable happiness sporadically. Why?

Connection. Connection to people you love, like, and discover you can trust. Connection to a community that is bigger than yourself. Through the Open Palms Ask, we foster connection by being open to our needs and the needs of others.

Jennifer Lytle is a bred, born, and raised Central Texan. She has been married to her husband for over fifteen years, and they have three sons and one daughter. Jennifer is a licensed marriage and family therapist and the founder of Joyful Journeys Counseling. Her international bestselling book, *The Perfectly Imperfect Family*, was released earlier this year. She has been published in several online magazines, including *Scary Mommy*, *Austin Fit Magazine*, *Choosing Therapy*, and *Care.com*. Follow her at joyfuljourneyscounseling.com or get your free copy of *Apples of Gold: A Family Communication Plan* to implement the suggestions in this chapter by using the QR code.

It's Not Your Fault, But It Is Your Problem

Melissa Kascak

A tiny flaw on a piece of 35mm film was the catalyst for one of the most powerful lessons in my life.

Developing film in the darkroom is a very fickle process. There are multiple tedious steps along the way where many things can go wrong. The film can't be exposed to even the slightest bit of light, or it will be completely ruined, and all your hard work will be destroyed. (This was the 1990s— before every phone had a camera and you could immediately see which shots you wanted to delete.) Take, for instance, feeding the unyielding 35mm film into a small plastic reel in complete and utter darkness, which is about as easy as it sounds. And that red light most people associate with a darkroom? That doesn't save you from the black void of film development.

When you're learning to develop film, it takes some finesse and some trial and error. You make mistakes and curse your fumbling fingers or whichever idiot opens the door while you're in the film room. And sometimes, the image you work so hard and long to perfect doesn't turn out the way you want because there's just a flaw in the film. Sometimes, something happens that is not your fault, but it becomes your problem.

When I was enlarging one particular negative, to my great frustration, no matter what I tried, I couldn't get it right. My favorite professor evaluated the situation and told me, "It's not your fault, but it is your problem."

His appraisal made me feel both better and worse. On one hand, I was relieved that it wasn't my fault that the error had occurred and I wasn't a buffoon who screwed up my own project. On the other, I now had to somehow figure out how to fix the embedded flaw in my negative.

Every once in a while, something will bring back the scent of the pungent chemicals from that darkroom. I can still see the layout in my mind's eye. I certainly don't remember the photo that I was working on or the actual flaw that made my professor offer those words, but that lesson stuck with me. It's become a guiding principle in both my personal and professional life, and it's part of the foundation that I share with clients today.

The Importance of This Lesson

Knowing that something isn't your fault feels warm and fuzzy, like a comfy old sweater that you've had for years. People love it when things aren't their fault; it's the ultimate release of culpability. *Hey, it wasn't my fault; there's nothing I can do.* There is validation: you couldn't have foreseen this issue, you couldn't really have planned for it; it's not something that you caused. So that must mean you're off the hook.

"It's not my fault" is one gigantic shrug, invoking a feeling of indifference.

But when you accept that even if something isn't your fault, it's still your problem, the onus is placed back on you. And here's the important part: the beauty of realizing that something is still your problem even if it wasn't your fault is that you take back your power to do something about it.

When you shift your mindset from blame to ownership, it's transformative. You move from passive to active, from helpless to capable.

When Life Throws You Curveballs

Plenty of times in life, there are things that are out of your control, things that you did nothing to cause. Things that are way bigger than a lousy flaw on your negative.

When my husband and I were ready to start a family and have babies, I could get pregnant at the drop of a hat, but I couldn't *stay* pregnant. It was heartbreaking. After lots of testing and poking and prodding, it turns out, it was no one's fault. Great news! But it was still our problem that we desperately wanted to fix more than anything. We followed the medical team's guidance with precision, and eventually, my body figured out how to stay pregnant.

Twice throughout my husband's 20+ year career with the same company, he was laid off from his job. It wasn't merit-based; both times the company was restructuring his department, and his position was eliminated. Each time was the worst timing possible; when I was roundly pregnant with our second child and again when the ink was still fresh on a pricier mortgage for a new home. My professor's words rang true in both instances. We didn't wait for the universe to provide—we teamed up to decrease expenses and hustled to get a new position even if it wasn't ideal and included more travel.

How This Lesson Can Help You

Let's be honest: "Not your fault but still your problem" doesn't always show up in such huge, life-altering ways. I'm sure there are many times in your life that you could consider something that isn't your fault. Your car got hit by someone else; a storm canceled your flight; your childcare falls through right before an important meeting; your child gets sick on a day with unmovable deadlines. None of those things are your fault, but they are your problem, and it's your cue to get busy solving.

Here's a simple three-step process I teach my clients for handling these situations:

1. **Acknowledge the reality**: Yes, this situation isn't fair or your fault.

2. **Shift to solution mode**: Instead of asking "Why did this happen to me?", focus on "What can I do now?" No shoulder shrugging allowed.

3. **Take immediate action**: Do one thing, however small, to address the problem.

As a personal and professional coach for working mothers facing stress and overwhelm, I help my clients foster the strength to address challenges, regardless of origin. I've witnessed remarkable transformations when women shift from feeling victimized by circumstances to actively shaping them. This mindset distinction between acknowledging something isn't your fault and recognizing you still have agency to address it becomes a cornerstone of their resilience.

This is a reality that working moms face constantly. A child's school unexpectedly closes. A presentation gets rescheduled at the last minute. A team member drops the ball on a project. None of these situations may be your fault, but as a working parent, they all become your problems to solve—sometimes even simultaneously.

Keeping this lesson in mind will make you feel less helpless when life throws these curveballs at you and tries to make you give up because it wasn't your fault. I don't know about you, but it pisses me off when something isn't my fault but now I have to clean up the mess. But even if you figure out who to blame—the reckless driver, Mother Nature, the other kids at school who got your kid sick—you are still the one who needs to deal with the fallout. It doesn't help to point fingers. What does help is to roll up your sleeves and get to work.

The Ripple Effect of Ownership

I like to think that we sleeve-rollers are setting an example for a brave new world of taking ownership. Just think of the other people who will be inspired by your approach of fixing problems that weren't your fault. Your kids will see you modeling this behavior and learn resilience is an option in the face of challenges. The other students aren't pulling their weight on a group project? You're still responsible for your portion of the grade. I'm planting the seed of taking ownership now when my boys are young so they can retain it and feel the courage to face things in their lives that they didn't cause.

I've been told that my can-do attitude has moved others to think, *What would Mel do in this situation?* Perhaps you will move coworkers to step in and help out or even own up and take the blame when it is their due if they see you setting the example of "it wasn't my fault but I'm fixing the problem" in your workplace. In professional settings, this attitude can transform team dynamics. When team members see a leader or colleague taking ownership of problems regardless of fault, it creates a culture of solution-seeking rather than blame-shifting. This approach builds trust, strengthens relationships, and ultimately leads to more effective problem-solving across the organization.

Of course, this principle doesn't mean you should shoulder every burden that comes your way. There are times when problems genuinely belong to someone else to solve. Sometimes you need to say, "Not my circus, not my monkeys," and cut your losses. Other times you will need to say, "Watch me train these monkeys anyway." The key is to evaluate which problems will impact your life, your work, or your overall goals if they are left unaddressed. Then you can decide if you'll step in regardless of to whom the circus belongs.

When my favorite photography professor told me all those years ago, "It's not your fault, but it is your problem," he taught me a lesson that has carried me through darkrooms and meeting rooms, through parenting challenges and professional hurdles. He gave me the understanding that solving problems—regardless of who or what caused them—is a kind of superpower. This mindset will make you more resilient, more resourceful, and ultimately more successful in the face of life's inevitable challenges. Because when you aren't confusing lack of fault with lack of agency, you realize it's never about taking blame; it's always about taking action.

Melissa Kascak is a certified personal and professional coach who specializes in helping working mothers find balance and fulfillment through evidence-based strategies and practical solutions. As Director of Operations for both Summit Success and Summit Press Publishers, she oversees strategic initiatives and drives organizational growth. With a BFA from the University of Connecticut, her creative background brings an artistic perspective to her problem-solving and personal development, allowing her to combine structure with innovation. Melissa lives in Newtown, Connecticut, with her husband and two young sons, where she models the work-life integration strategies she teaches her clients.

For practical tools to tackle problems you didn't create, scan or visit fityourselfin.com/response-ability-guide to access your complimentary *Response-Ability Guide*.

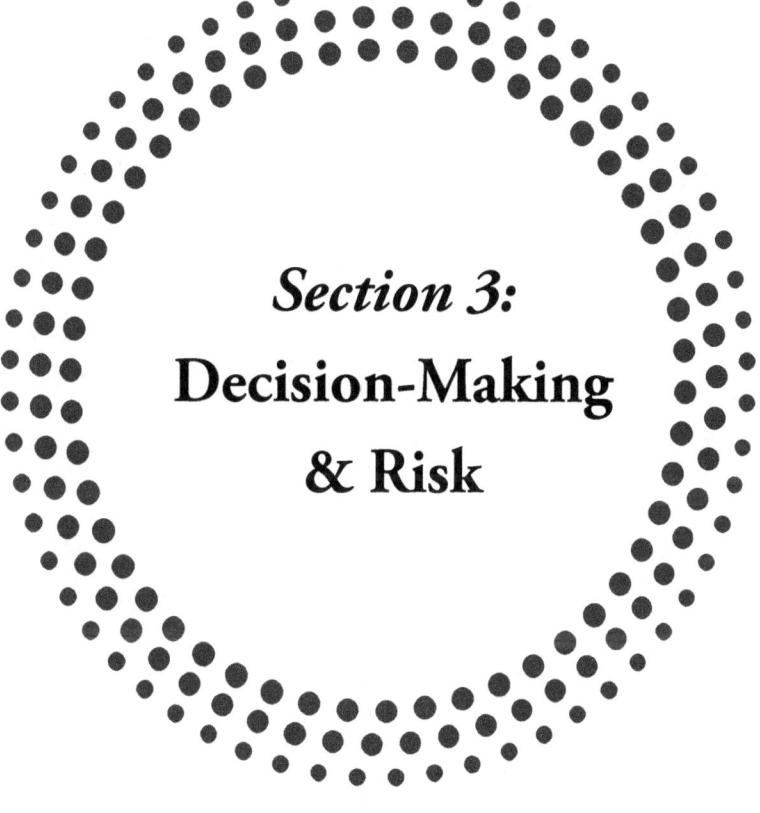

Section 3:
Decision-Making
& Risk

Take Calculated Risks

Ann Sheybani

I'm a student of risk. I'm constantly trying to figure out which ones I should take to grow and which I shouldn't because I lack information and stand to lose something of value. I'm afraid of getting it wrong because I know how easily I can delude myself when I want the reward.

Case in point.

When I moved to my husband's home country, I imagined exotic escapades to write home about, a close-knit family where I could finally belong, a buttress for my shaky marriage, and a life utterly different from my miserable parents'. What I got instead was isolation, cultural whiplash, and the dawning recognition that I was in way over my head. Cue the nosedive from bad to worse.

I ignored all the warnings about Iran. The travel agent—an Iranian woman with an armful of gold bangles—told me I wasn't "cut out for the life." My mother, who was married to a mean alcoholic, cried about how "they treat their women." Even my Vietnamese friend, who had risked everything to come to America, couldn't understand why I'd move in the opposite direction, straight into a war-torn, third-world country.

I even shrugged when the Iranian customs official confiscated my American passport, making me an official extension of my husband with no independent rights. I was convinced I'd be fine because I had no imagination for any other outcome. I was angry, resentful, drunk on youthful hubris, and desperate for love—all of which left me blind.

Risk involves calculation—a clear-eyed assessment of potential gains weighed against possible losses. On the other hand, recklessness skips the math and jumps straight to the action, fueled by emotion, impulse, or the desperate need to prove something. (My move to Iran had all those earmarks.) Risk says, "This might not work, but I've considered what happens if it doesn't." Recklessness says, "This will be awesome!" and leaves it at that.

Without calculation, you're not taking risks; you're gambling, betting the house on sheer luck. And more often than you might expect, you lose. Not just you—others get hurt in the fallout.

I gambled with my future, safety, and, eventually, my children's well-being. I upended my husband's life, which was hard to forgive myself for. I hadn't calculated; I had romanticized. I hadn't assessed; I had fantasized. The price tag for that kind of recklessness proved too high for everyone involved. In other words, I left bodies on the field.

Yet, I have a strange fudge ripple of recklessness running through me still, at least in the physical world.

I felt it on Denali as I balanced on a knife's edge with 6,000-foot drops on either side. The wind whipped my clothes, and my body quaked with the visceral knowledge that one false move meant plummeting to my death. I'd never bumped up against my mortality quite that way. Sure, I trained. I prepared. But I hadn't truly assessed the dangers, let alone the rewards. I saw it again while traversing the Gouter Ridge of Mont Blanc, feeling like a ceramic pin in a high-speed bowling alley. I'd read plenty of alpine adventure books rife with such setups. I got how easily tragedy can strike. In both cases, I had leaped before I looked. (I mean, *really looked*.)

I'll often leap before I look because I would never do a damn thing if I sat down for a hot minute and thought about it. Maybe it's because I considered my parents so fearful, so trapped by the constraints of their era. I am where I am because I've said yes to opportunities or invitations without any assessment. I suppose I have faith that I'll figure it out and be alright.

Yet here's the contradiction that defines me: I consider myself highly risk averse. I'm not into jeopardizing money, my reputation, or my time. If failure is an option, I'll think long and hard before I make a move, which can cramp one's growth as a business owner. Try committing to a line of action when constantly looking for a safety hatch or a ripcord provision.

When guarantees are anything but forthcoming. Often, the default is to do nothing, to play it safe and small.

I watch others calculate risk every day. Someone wants to write or publish a book but is unsure if it's the right time. I can practically hear the wheels turn in their head—*maybe I'll choose the wrong topic, or start something that I won't finish, or spend time on something that won't get me what I want, or I'll reveal myself to be a fake (or moron)*. I used to believe that people pulled back from the precipice because they didn't trust me when, really, they were questioning their own penchant for recklessness. Had they thought things through?

This constant tension between action and inaction creates a mental tug-of-war. I'll beat myself up for being cautious when business friends take massive action and succeed. Then I'll all but gloat when others fail, telling myself I would never take such "unnecessary risks." Playing it safe becomes the perfect justification for my inaction.

The experts don't help. Seth Godin says, "The cost of being wrong is less than the cost of doing nothing." But I see plenty of business casualties that suggest otherwise.

Back and forth I go: jump—no, think—just do it—consider the variables....

I love spreadsheets that allow me to calculate risk. Plug in the numbers—no emotion, magical thinking, or false hope—and let them tell me what to do. Bill Perkins, former hedge fund manager and author of *Die With Zero*, offered one that allows you to figure out how to spend your money without hitting zero before you die. I like that sort of guarantee because, when push comes to shove, I'm terrified of failure and loss. Of ending up alone because I've made an unforgivable mistake and living in a cardboard box. Of leaving bodies on the field.

J.K. Rowling helped me reframe my relationship with risk and failure. In her Harvard commencement address, she said: "It is impossible to live without failing at something unless you live so cautiously that you might as well not have lived at all. In which case, you fail by default."

Rowling described her own spectacular failure—jobless, a lone parent, "as poor as it is possible to be in modern Britain without being homeless." She explained how that rock-bottom moment stripped away everything inessential and forced her to direct all her energy toward the only thing that mattered to her: writing.

"Had I really succeeded at anything else," she said, "I might never have found the determination to succeed in the one arena I believed I truly belonged."

Rowling wasn't advocating recklessness. She wasn't suggesting we throw ourselves headlong into disaster just to see what happens. What she described was the value of calculated risk—of pursuing something that matters deeply enough that the potential failure feels worth it.

This was a hard concept for me to swallow. I've treated failure as an enemy to avoid at all costs, so the idea that I should not only accept its possibility but also get comfortable with it felt counterintuitive.

But Rowling was onto something profound: "Failure taught me things about myself that I could have learned no other way. I discovered that I had a strong will and more discipline than I had suspected; I also found out that I had friends whose value was truly above the price of rubies."

When I think about my failures—not just the Iran debacle but the unfinished manuscripts, the business ventures that fizzled, and the relationships that imploded—I realize that each one revealed something about myself I couldn't have discovered otherwise. Each one strengthened muscles I didn't know I had and made me face stuff about myself I didn't like. My successes have done the same.

Getting comfortable with failure doesn't mean courting it. It means understanding that failure isn't the opposite of success; it's a component of it. It's reconnaissance—valuable intelligence from the frontlines of your life.

Surviving failure—spectacular failure—allowed me to start my own business despite knowing that 90% fail within three years. Spending money, hiring people, taking on projects without guaranteed outcomes—all of it feels like spinning a gigantic roulette wheel. But I can better distinguish between the wheel of recklessness and the wheel of calculated risk at this stage of the game.

Risk is necessary precisely because it forces growth. It pushes us beyond comfort into possibility, demanding that we develop new skills, perspectives, and resilience. Intense focus.

The calculation matters—not just the assessment of practical dangers, though that's important. The deeper calculation involves knowing what you value enough to risk failure.

J.K. Rowling risked failure for writing. She bet everything on the thing that mattered most to her, and that bet—informed by passion and purpose—paid off spectacularly.

In my own life, I've started applying this framework. When considering a new business venture last year, instead of my usual paralysis, I asked myself: "What's the worst outcome I can live with? What's the best outcome worth risking for?" This clarity helped me take a calculated risk that has become my most profitable program.

The truth about risk is that we can't avoid it. Even if we try to play it completely safe, we risk regret, stagnation, and, as Rowling put it, "failing by default." Our only real choice is whether our risks will be calculated or reckless.

I've found that the sweet spot isn't avoiding risk altogether or diving in without thought—it's that careful space in between where we weigh what matters against what it might cost.

Risk, properly calculated, is the art of knowing which leaps are worth taking and then finding the courage to jump.

Ann Sheybani is the director of Summit Press Publishers. As a certified sales and marketing coach, Harvard-trained writer, content developer, best-selling author, and publisher of numerous award-winning books, she knows which stories get results and which do not. Keep your readers enthralled, and they will look for ways to work with you or invite you into their world. Ann Sheybani, a fan of risk minimization—particularly for writers—created a free guide entitled *Avoid the 5 BIG Mistakes Most Coaches, Consultants, and Speakers Make When Writing a Book,* which you can access at https://summitsuccess.lpages.co/5-mistakes/ or by scanning the QR code.

Chase It Down the Street

James F. Twyman

There is a moment—fleeting, electric—when inspiration hits. It arrives like a whisper in the chest or a sudden rush behind the eyes. In that moment, you feel the full force of clarity: *a book you must write, a conversation you must have, a project you must begin.* And then, almost as quickly, it fades.

What happens next determines everything.

For most people, the moment of inspiration is followed by the impulse to plan. We reach for our notebooks, our whiteboards, our software. We draw timelines and create steps. We research. We refine. We organize.

And then... nothing happens. The spark dims. The clarity wanes. The life-changing idea slowly becomes just another item on a growing to-do list. This is a call to break that cycle.

I've never been a planner—for whatever reason. Maybe I'm too impulsive or impatient, but behind both of these, there is another quality that has been my go-to for as long as I can remember: I'm not afraid of failure. I'm grateful for the many successes that have shaped my life, but I can also claim many, many failures along the way—projects or ideas I launched that fell flat. But every bolt of inspiration that *did* lead to a successful outcome urged me on, and many more followed. My lack of fear wasn't a detriment but a childlike quality that led to a life filled with adventure and success.

Here's one example: In 2001, I learned how to bend spoons with my mind. (Yes, you read that correctly.) It was a bit of a novelty, but it usually worked, and everyone who saw me perform this "trick" wanted to learn how to do it themselves. You need to know that online courses were just beginning to be released at this time. I was a relatively well-known author at that time but by no means a "front row" authority. A friend suggested I write down the process I had mastered and send it out to my email list—a four-part document that took people through the steps of what I called "miracle-mindedness." These days, online courses are accompanied by videos, Zoom classes, and a wide assortment of other elements. Not mine. Those were tools that had yet to become accessible. "The Spoonbender Course" was around 1,500 words in length, and that was it.

I decided to charge only $25 for the course, figuring that the low cost and strange content would intrigue people enough to give it a try. Everyone I knew told me to plan it out, get my ducks in order, hire a team of marketing professionals, and make sure I knew what I was doing. None of these things felt in alignment, so I ignored them all. I wrote a few short emails describing the course and sent them to my email list.

Within a week, "The Spoonbender Course" brought in approximately $500,000. Not only that, but it was like breaking the four-minute mile. Every other author I knew began planning their own online course, figuring if that "Twyman guy" could do it, they could too. They began planning their strategy, arranging their thoughts, taking notes, and hiring the strategists they needed to match my Cinderella success story.

But none of them came close to the success of my course on bending a spoon with the mind and miracle-mindedness.

So, let's begin by looking at the traps that get in the way of achieving the success we know we deserve.

What Does It Mean to "Chase It Down the Street"?

Imagine your inspiration is like a child who just learned how to run. The moment she bolts down the street, your only job is to *run after her*. Not to build a map. Not to buy running shoes. Not to consult a coach.

Just go.

"Chase it down the street" means that when an idea lands, you move. You put it into motion. You write the first paragraph.

You post the video. You send the email. Not tomorrow. Not after a strategy session. *Now.*

The Inner Tools of Activation

To live this way, you don't need to be fearless. You don't need to be perfect. You just need to cultivate a few key inner tools:

1. **Self-Trust**

   Your intuition is not a novelty—it's your compass. When something resonates, act. Trust that your inner "yes" is enough reason to begin. The logic can catch up later.

   The more you listen to and act on your intuition, the stronger it becomes. It's like a muscle: use it, and it grows. Ignore it, and it atrophies. Each time you follow that subtle nudge—no matter how small—you deepen your relationship with your own guidance system.

2. **Tolerating the Unknown**

   The unknown is not your enemy—it's your studio, your temple, your training ground. Most people avoid it because they associate uncertainty with danger. But something beautiful happens in the space of not knowing: your creativity comes alive. Possibility breathes.

3. **Letting Go of Outcome**

   When you activate from inspiration, let go of where it has to lead. The point isn't to guarantee success—

it's to stay in motion. Progress is more important than perfection.

When you free yourself from outcome, you become more experimental, more courageous, more present. You try things. You listen more. You enjoy the unfolding. This is where the magic happens—not in the perfectly executed plan, but in the alive, unpredictable process of showing up.

4. **Courage to Be Seen**

   Courage to be seen means releasing the image of who you think you're supposed to be. It means letting the truth be more important than the presentation. People are drawn to what's alive, not what's flawless. It's the crack in the voice, the shaky hand, the unfiltered word that makes your offering real.

The Outer Tools of Activation

Alongside inner alignment, you can build a world around you that supports fast activation.

1. **The One-Touch Rule**

   When an idea comes, take one immediate action. Record a note, send a message, or make a sketch. This keeps the energy alive.

The key is to strike while the idea is still warm. A single gesture of action tells your system, "This matters." It shifts the idea from the mental realm into the material one. This small move can create a ripple of motivation that leads naturally to the next step.

2. **Create a Launch Habit**

The habit doesn't need to feel heroic. It can be subtle and simple: lighting a candle, opening a blank page, pressing record. The important part is honoring the moment. Protect that window like you would a sacred appointment. Because it is.

3. **Keep Tools Handy**

Creative energy is fragile in its early stages. When an idea visits, you want the path from thought to action to be as short as possible. Having your tools visible and ready removes the friction that causes delay. You don't need a perfect setup—you need accessibility.

4. **Build a Support Circle**

Surround yourself with people who value activation over analysis. Let them know when you're acting on something new. Their energy will amplify yours.

Let your circle hold you accountable for *doing*, not just dreaming. Share your sparks of inspiration as they arise, even before you have it all figured out. You'll be surprised how often someone says, "Go for it," or "I had a similar thought," or "Let me help." Their encouragement becomes the wind at your back.

Why This Works

Inspiration is perishable. It has a shelf life. It's a wave you either ride or watch crash. The more you hesitate, the more distant it feels.

But when you act immediately, even in small ways, you catch the current. You stay connected to the pulse of the idea. You don't just honor the inspiration—you join it.

Inspiration is like fire: it wants oxygen. Activation is the oxygen.

Inspiration doesn't just come to the most talented but to the most open. It knocks on the door of anyone willing to listen. But only those who act become its vessel. The moment you move with it, you become part of a creative flow much larger than yourself. You're not just expressing something; you're participating in a living current.

Another reason this works is that it bypasses the inner critic. When you move fast, there's less time for judgment to creep in. You stay ahead of your resistance. You create a pattern of aliveness where action and insight feed each other. And over time, that becomes your new normal—a state where ideas don't die on the vine but ripen through your willingness to move.

Ultimately, this works because it mirrors the natural world. Seeds don't wait for certainty. Rivers don't check maps. The sun rises without asking who will notice. Life moves; when you move with it, you re-enter your rightful place as a co-creator of something alive, wild, and real.

What About Discipline? What About Excellence?

This approach isn't anti-discipline. It's not about sloppy work. It's about *beginning* in motion. Planning and refining can still happen—but they come *after* the spark is alive.

Once the wheel is turning, you can shape it. Edit it. Polish it. But you can't steer a car that's parked.

Inspiration—Activate—Refine. That's the rhythm.

Final Thoughts

You already have everything you need. The guidance is inside you. The tools are in your hands. The map appears *as you move*.

Don't wait to be certain. Don't wait to be qualified. Don't wait for permission.

You saw it. You felt it. That's enough.

Now, go chase it down.

James Twyman is an Episcopal priest and Franciscan friar. He is the author of twenty-four books, including the *New York Times* best-seller *The Moses Code*. The founder of Namaste Village, an interfaith community in Ajijic, Mexico, he is known around the world as the Peace Troubadour for the peace concerts he has performed in many of the world's most dangerous war zones. Choose one project, idea, or inspiration to act upon today—big or small—without knowing how you'll publish, distribute, or share the information, and start chasing it down the street. To learn more about James, scan the code below.

Always Be Looking to Replace Yourself

Kristen Arnold

I f your business can't run without you, you don't own it—it owns you.

Most founders push back. Isn't being irreplaceable the point?

No. That's ego talking, not strategy.

True business builders don't create dependencies—they eliminate them. You haven't built a company if your business depends on you for daily operations and decisions. You've built yourself a job with extra steps.

And that job will become your prison.

Founders in the "messy middle" are stuck. They're smart. They work insanely hard. But they're trapped making every decision while the team waits for direction and growth stalls.

The problem isn't their team or their delegation skills; it's their core systems. Specifically, it's their inability to replace themselves in critical business functions.

My Journey from Job Holder to Business Builder

I didn't always understand this. My career path from corporate HR to mergers and acquisitions to entrepreneur to freelance project manager to COO of a 40-person, $10 million business taught me this lesson the hard way.

I remember sitting at my desk at 11 p.m., answering "urgent" emails about decisions that, frankly, someone else should have been able to make. My team was talented and worked hard, but they were trained to bring everything to me.

Why? Because I hadn't made myself replaceable. I'd made myself the hub—and was paying the price for it.

The business was growing, but I was the bottleneck. Every decision, every problem, every new initiative ran through me. My ego loved feeling needed. I couldn't step away without everything slowing down or falling apart.

I was building a job, not a business. And the stakes were high: growth had plateaued, burnout loomed, and we were all paying what I now call the "invisible tax" of founder dependency—where execution slows because everyone's waiting on one person.

The Advice That Changed Everything

It was during this breaking point that I recalled the advice that would transform my approach: "Always be looking to replace yourself."

It came from a mentor who had grown himself through various businesses. I initially bristled at the suggestion. Replace myself? But nobody understands the ins and outs like I see them. Nobody cares about it like I do. Nobody has the unique combination of skills and experience that I bring.

"That's exactly the problem," my mentor explained. "As long as you're irreplaceable, you can never grow beyond your personal capacity."

The mindset shift was profound. I realized I'd been playing the wrong game entirely. Instead of measuring my value by how necessary I was, I needed to measure it by how unnecessary I could make myself.

This wasn't about diminishing my role. It was about evolving it from essential operator to strategic architect.

What Business Builders Actually Do

Business builders don't just delegate tasks; they transfer ownership.

This requires three critical skills that most founders struggle to develop:

First, business builders hire people smarter than themselves in key areas. This seems obvious, but it's psychologically challenging. Your ego wants to be the smartest person in the room. Your insecurity whispers that you'll be exposed as a fraud. Push past it. A true business builder's strength isn't in knowing everything—it's in building a team that collectively knows more than any individual could.

Second, business builders practice the discipline of not stepping in. This is harder than it sounds. When you see someone doing something differently than you would—even if the outcome will be the same—the impulse to grab the wheel is overwhelming. Resist it. Let them drive. Let them find their own way. This isn't abdication; it's calculated restraint.

Third, business builders understand the growth paradox: you become stronger when you make yourself "unnecessary." Something unexpected happened as I systematically replaced myself in operations, client management, and even strategic planning. I found higher-value work that only I could do— work I never had time for when I was busy being "essential" to everything else.

I replaced myself as project manager by promoting someone who brought fresh perspectives and ultimately improved our systems. I replaced myself in client meetings by training account managers who built stronger relationships than I ever could. Eventually, I even replaced myself in most strategic decisions by developing a leadership team that could collectively think for themselves and work through challenges.

Each time I handed something off, I made room for something bigger—profit, peace, purpose.

The Business Builder's Blueprint

This approach works regardless of your business size or industry but requires intention. Here's how to implement it:

For founders, start by replacing yourself in these critical functions, in this order:

1. **Day-to-day operations:** These consume time but rarely require your unique talents.

2. **Customer service and support:** Someone else can solve problems just as well as you.

3. **Project/product delivery:** Build systems others can run without your constant input.

4. **Sales conversations:** Yes, even this can be systematized and transferred.

Leave vision and culture for last; that's your zone.

For operators and team members, become irreplaceable by making yourself replaceable. Sounds counterintuitive, right? But the most valuable team members aren't those who hoard knowledge and become bottlenecks themselves. They're the ones who document, systematize, and teach others what they know—freeing themselves to take on greater challenges.

Overcoming Resistance

If making yourself replaceable is so powerful, why don't more founders do it? Because it triggers deep psychological resistance:

The identity crisis comes first. When your self-worth is tied to being needed, making yourself unnecessary feels like self-sabotage. You've been "the person who does the work" for so long that becoming "the person who builds the business" feels like a betrayal of your expertise.

Then there's the control dilemma. Business builders must trust others with their vision—letting go of exactly how things get done to focus on whether the right things get done. This requires shifting from controlling processes to establishing outcomes.

Finally, the perfectionism trap derails even the best intentions. "They won't do it exactly like I would" becomes the justification for staying involved in everything. And you're right—they won't do it exactly like you. Sometimes, they'll do it worse. Sometimes, they'll do it better. Either way, the business grows only when you let go.

I struggled with all three of these mindset blocks. What finally helped me overcome them was realizing that my identity shouldn't be tied to what I do but to what I build. My value wasn't in being needed today but in creating something that could outlast my daily involvement.

Long-Term Benefits

When you commit to making yourself replaceable, the rewards extend far beyond operational efficiency. You create a fundamentally different kind of business—and life.

Freedom becomes real, not theoretical. I don't mean just taking vacations (though that happens too). I'm talking about the freedom to choose where your time and energy go each day. When you're no longer the bottleneck for every decision, you gain the space to think strategically instead of reactively. You can focus on the next horizon rather than today's fires.

Your business becomes exponentially more valuable—both to you and to others. A business dependent on its founder is worth substantially less than one with distributed leadership and operational independence. Whether you want to sell eventually or create a reliable asset, a business that runs without you is worth multiples more than one that collapses in your absence.

Perhaps most importantly, you discover your highest and best use. When you're no longer consumed by tasks others could do, you find where your unique talents truly create leverage. For me, this meant focusing on strategic partnerships and new market development—work I genuinely loved but never had time for when I was the bottleneck for daily decisions.

The ultimate outcome is a business that serves your life, not the other way around. You built your business for a reason—probably some combination of impact, income, and independence. Making yourself replaceable is how you achieve those goals rather than sacrificing them on the altar of being needed.

Building Your Legacy, Not Just Your Job

Your business will only grow to the extent that you can make yourself replaceable. This isn't just advice for scaling—it's the fundamental mindset shift between working a job and building a legacy.

Ask yourself honestly: Are you building a business or working a complicated job?

If you recognize yourself in any part of this chapter—if you're still the bottleneck, if decisions stall without you, if stepping away causes your chest to tighten—then it's time to start replacing yourself.

Begin with one area. Just one. Where are you currently essential that you don't need to be? What knowledge exists only in your head? What decisions always come to you that someone else could make with the right guidance?

Identify that area, document what you know, train someone else, and—this is the hard part—actually let them take over. Not with your constant supervision. Not with you swooping in to fix mistakes. Actually, let go.

This is how you evolve from founder to business builder. This is how you create something that lasts beyond your daily involvement. This is how you build a business that grows beyond the limitations of your time, energy, and capacity.

Always be looking to replace yourself. It's the only path to building a business that outlasts you.

Kristen Arnold, founder of Business Builders United, helps visionary founders build teams that run the business without them—freeing their time, protecting their vision, and scaling smarter. A former freelance project manager turned three-time COO, Kristen spent two decades inside seven- and eight-figure companies, leading $5 million launches, managing more than 40 remote teams, and turning chaotic operations into high-performance machines. With 20 years of battle-tested experience, Kristen created the Lean Operator Lab to give founders the strategic right-hand support they need—and to mentor the next generation of operators who lead with clarity, ownership, and results.

A sought-after speaker and strategist, Kristen is known for helping founders scale without becoming the bottleneck—and for building businesses that grow in freedom without losing their heart or soul.

Learn how to build a business that runs without you and scale with freedom at businessbuildersunited.com, where Kristen Arnold helps visionary founders create high-performance teams.

Section 4:
Authentic Leadership & Purpose

You Must Stand for Something

Jill James

You've decided to start a company. Or maybe you already have one. If you're a founder who came from corporate, you've positioned your company's value around saving time or money for your customers, assuming they will reward you with profitable sales.

Guess what? Nobody cares.

Today's shoppers—consumers and businesses—want more than efficiency from the companies they support. Most buyers want to spend with brands aligned with their beliefs and world-views. This isn't just an American phenomenon. The World Economic Forum tracks a global metric called Stakeholder Capitalism. Since 2021, the measure of people who expect a brand to be aligned and have a stance on making their lives better has gone from 51% to over 70%.[1] In the United States, similar measures have made an incredible jump to include 82% of consumers in 2024.

This shift represents a fundamental change in how business value is perceived. While corporate environments often reduce success to a single metric—profit—today's marketplace demands more. Consumers aren't just buying products or services; they're investing in companies whose values reflect their own. This means that the very thing many corporate environments discourage—having a distinctive voice and stance—has become essential for business success. The question isn't whether you should stand for something but how you deliver value by executing in alignment with your values.

If you are a business owner raised in corporate, building a business around beliefs and values will feel strange. It's certainly not what you're taught in business school. As an employee, you were asked to optimize profits and choices for the interests of an abstract "shareholder." But in your own business, you're the shareholder. What are your interests?

Building your own business allows you to define success beyond pure profit metrics—to create something meaningful that reflects your values and vision. Yet standing for something isn't a thing you can workshop or pull out of the air based on customer feedback. In my work with thousands of founders,

---

1 Andrea Willige. "People Prefer Brands with Aligned Corporate Purpose and Values." World Economic Forum, 17 Dec. 2021, www.weforum.org/stories/2021/12/people-prefer-brands-with-aligned-corporate-purpose-and-values/.

I've learned that building the foundation of a company that stands for something has to come from your personal beliefs or a change you want to make in the world. And that change must be something deeper than making yourself wealthy, even though earning money and improving your financial well-being will be a big motivator for starting a company.

I came to understand this principle through my own business-building journey. I started my company in 2015 when I was seven months pregnant. I had been proud of my always-on, 80-hour week schedule since my 20s. However, the all-in demands of a venture-backed business did not work with being the primary caregiver to my child.

The restrictions on my time forced me to get creative. Many of my mentors at the time were married men with partners who shouldered more than 50% of the effort with their kids, freeing them up to travel to client sites every week. I knew I couldn't work like that, so I was faced with a challenge: How do I make this business work with these known constraints?

Boundaries can be a good thing. I started working remotely and required that approach for my engagements. I was upfront about what was possible, when I could work, and when we would be closed. I didn't know it then, but I had established a centering principle for my business: we will always show up to care for our loved ones.

This principle became the foundation of my business model and allowed me to connect with my ideal clients. By two years into my business, I had worked with different founders and

companies, from Fortune 1000 brands to individuals contemplating a leap to self-employment. I could see clearly that
entrepreneurial moms didn't have the luxury of putting their
heads down and working 80 hours a week. They valued support, flexibility, and efficiency. And there were a lot of them.
Many women trying to figure out how to make life work with a
leadership career were opting out of corporate to start companies. As an experienced operator, I knew I had the skills to help
them define what they wanted and build that company. And
I knew that more companies that existed with a flexible leadership mindset would lead to more flexible jobs for even more
caregivers. And the way to do this was to build smaller, self-
funded companies where these women kept ownership control.

Staying true to my centering principles made me realize
that ownership control was essential to maintaining a values-driven business approach. Now, ten years into working
with early-stage, self-funded businesses, I'm committed to
helping founders define and build their own CEO playbook.
If you want to maintain the integrity of your centering principles, you must keep ownership of your company. In most
cases, you'll be self-funded. That means you need to focus at
least 60% of your time on work that you love, that drives customer relationships and sales revenue. This is not the venture
playbook.

Purpose isn't separate from profit. Purpose-driven founders must be financially successful in building small and mid-
sized businesses. In his book *The Passion Economy*, author and

podcaster Adam Davidson discusses finding and building a niche business. Most of us start companies because we have a "yes and" mindset—accepting multiple, complementary motivations. We want to improve our financial security, solve a meaningful problem, or change our work.

This dual motivation is precisely why centering principles are so crucial to your business strategy. Jessica Alba, co-founder of The Honest Company, wrote a book about how vital her centering principles were to guiding what The Honest Company would and would not do. A centering principle is a non-negotiable fact about how you want to run your company. It's a "we will always" statement. Centering principles help us define how we want to grow, which customers are aligned with us, what kinds of people we need on our teams, what partners we work with, and why we get up every day, even when things get challenging.

In my work, the founders with strong centering principles have an easier time defining what's for them and what's not. Their teams can anticipate a yes and a no. They can make decisions without constantly relying on the founder as a bottleneck. Marketing is clearer because we know who our aligned customers are, what they expect from us as a brand and company, and how to build products and communities around them. Decision-making is faster. Yeses and noes are clearer. And saying no doesn't come with FOMO because you know the option you chose to forego is not meant for you or your business.

Let me illustrate centering principles with real examples from my clients.

A hair extension business: We want a fully ethical supply chain that financially benefits those who contribute to making and using our products at every point.

A production company: We want to create industry access for individuals who don't have natural connections by making space for trainees on every project so they can build their list of credits.

A law firm: We fight for individuals who have lost loved ones to corporate negligence in product design and manufacturing.

If you had this clarity, how would it change how you made decisions in your business?

The unexpected benefit of growth driven by centering principles is that you attract higher-value customers and grow with greater predictability. In fact, many of my clients grow faster than they expected because they're speaking clearly to one customer set with one clearly defined product or service. Their effort and investment are aimed at solving real, valuable problems, and customers and clients are motivated to support and amplify.

You might wonder why this approach isn't widely adopted and what makes it so difficult to implement. Self-funding isn't what gets the headlines in "sexy" business press. TechCrunch doesn't exist to tell the story of someone who grew steadily for 15 years to build a $25 million business. Venture capital is about quickly building toward a high asset valuation that can be offered for sale, not developing a company with long-term sustainable profits. And we like eye-popping headlines about big investments in plucky individuals with hero stories.

In reality, 98% of businesses never get venture or equity investor funding. And of the 2% that do, only about 2% of that funding goes to female-founded companies. (It jumps to 20% if you have a male co-founder.)[2] If you can't access traditional venture capital, why are you following a VC-driven playbook?

In a self-funded business, you'll need to prove its viability before traditional lending institutions will help you. You'll need to be in business for at least two years to get an SBA loan or a conventional line of credit. That means you must find customers who want to buy from you now to fund your business from sales. And that gets easier when you can tell your early customers what you stand for and deliver on that promise. It doesn't require an HR department or a mission leader. It's you leading a company designed around a self-motivating goal.

The long-term benefits of this approach are transformative. By designing your business around defined centering principles, you will build a business you want to run now and later. When you're having a day where you feel beaten up, you have a reason to rest and try again—something to fight for. You want to make time to work on your business because you

2 PitchBook-NVCA. "Q4 2024 PitchBook-NVCA Venture Monitor." National Venture Capital Association, 27 Jan. 2025, nvca.org/document/q4-2024-pitchbook-nvca-venture-monitor-2/.

know your efforts go toward solving a bigger problem. Having clear alignment in your products, pricing, customers, and team elevates your impact.

Ultimately, the most successful founders understand this fundamental truth: you and your company must stand for something. When you build from that foundation, everything else—your marketing, hiring, product development, and growth—becomes not just more authentic but more effective. And in today's market, where consumers increasingly demand alignment with their values, standing for something isn't just good ethics—it's good business.

Jill James is a business strategist who has helped thousands of self-funded business owners define and build companies with impact and profits. She has used her experience on Wall Street and in Silicon Valley and her MBA from the University of Chicago to help founders build and run companies on their own terms. To date, six of her clients have been named to the Inc. 5000. She lives in Los Angeles with her kiddo. Ready to define your centering principles? Download the free workbook based on our work with thousands of clients here.

Don't Follow Other People's Food Rules

Iman Sheybani

When I first moved to Spain almost a decade ago, my digestion took a major hit. It might have been the fact that shortly after the move, I gave birth to my daughter and subsequently faced a torrent of hormonal changes hitherto unknown. Within those first six postpartum months, I couldn't eat an egg without feeling like tiny daggers were attacking my insides. A plate of spaghetti turned into a bludgeoning brick in my stomach. The bowl of lentil soup that was supposed to give me the fiber and protein I needed to power through a day of solo parenting instead had me dialing the doctor and calling for childcare reinforcements.

I had no idea what was going on. I had always considered myself a healthy eater. And by almost anyone's estimation, I was. My favorite food had always been a big bowl of salad with veggies, nuts, and perhaps some roasted chickpeas for a kick. I had never been a big fan of cakes or chocolate-flavored anything, preferring to pick the fruit off a cream tart if that were an option. I could never relate when people agonized over their sugar habit or their dislike of vegetables, and I had no taste for sodas or artificial foods. I naturally gravitated to flavorful, whole foods. So, I really could not understand why my digestive system was turning against me.

I tried what felt like a thousand different things to address the digestive pain, including a visit to the gastroenterologist—who just so happened to be a distant in-law—leaving the office only with an understanding of what it really means to stick something "where the sun don't shine." Inspired by the latest Internet trend, I tried cutting out wheat and dairy. I was convinced I must also have inflammation. Instead of the pain subsiding, I just withered away, unable to find a viable alternative to bread in my tiny village and not feeling that I had the time, space, or energy to cook. I resorted to eating rice cakes with almond butter, hoping I wouldn't get hit with the adult version of colic.

I spent about a year like this until I finally fell upon an explanation that made sense. During an afternoon spent Googling my symptoms, I was directed to a blog about Ayurveda. I wasn't sure what this 5,000-year-old Indian science could offer me that other forms of medicine, holistic as they may be, couldn't. There in the blog post were all the words associated with my experience over the past year: pain, constipation, anxiety, fear (re: baby eating leaves near a poisonous Mediterranean plant), gas, bloating, cracking joints, weight loss, amenorrhea, debilitating cold. These things could be exacerbated by major life changes, pregnancy and childbirth, constant movement, disturbed sleep, poor posture, erratic eating, cold foods, raw foods, dry foods, and general undernourishment. I ticked off the boxes in my head and felt a jolt of excitement that told me that if the causes and symptoms could be so perfectly encapsulated, then perhaps so too could the solution.

What the article recommended for disturbed "Vata," a term I didn't yet know but would soon be devoting hours of study to, was a range of food and lifestyle prescriptions. Firstly, I would have to eat three meals a day every day at the same time. The food would have to be warm and freshly cooked with light, easy-to-digest ingredients. Think chicken soups and one-pot stews. Rice cakes were out. Actual cooked rice with butter or oil drizzled on top was back in. Spices such as cinnamon, ginger, cumin, turmeric, and anise should be incorporated to kindle the digestive fire. Salads, raw fruit, and cruciferous vegetables were out for the time being. Aha! I could now see why that plate of broccoli almost had me hospitalized. It didn't matter the fiber, vitamin, or mineral content or how healthy everyone says it is; given my condition at that particular time, in that particular place, in that particular season, broccoli operated more like a poisonous dart in my system rather than an elixir of health. I began to understand that other people's food rules may not always apply.

I experimented with the article's recommendations, just as I tell my clients to do when they receive their list of Ayurvedic guidelines. I saw that, within days of paying attention to when I was eating, how I was eating (i.e., in a chair instead of grazing at the counter), and the qualities of the food I was eating, I began to actually enjoy food again. The pain subsided. I started having regular bowel movements. My daughter's sneezes stopped setting off screeching alarm bells in my head. Shelving the salads for those few months and switching to sautéed vegetables instead, incorporating sweeter desserts like creamy, spiced rice pudding and stewed fruit, and avoiding iced drinks like they were the plague completely transformed my daily experience. I was smitten. I had to know more about Ayurveda.

Soon after, I formally trained to become an Ayurvedic Health Counselor. I felt that if Ayurveda could solve problems that that invasive gastroenterologist couldn't, I had better get to studying. As novices to the science, we were after rules. "What does Ayurveda say about morning smoothies?" "What does Ayurveda say about almond vs. oat milk?" "What does Ayurveda say about steak dinners?" One of the principles our teacher continuously drilled into our heads was that there was no one Ayurvedic principle that could be universally applied. Everything depended on the person. And no principle could be applied to that person as a blanket rule for their lifetime. No, no. Food rules change over the course of that person's life, depending on their age and the wear and tear on their body. In fact, recommendations changed over the course of that person's year, let alone life, transitioning in line with the seasons they experienced. We couldn't give the same recommendations to a person living in the desert of Arizona that we would to someone in Stockholm, even if they were experiencing the same symptoms. To make it even more complex, recommendations were to shift according to the time of day. What might be an excellent food choice for a particular person at noon has a whole other impact at 8 p.m., when the body is preparing for rest.

If you browse the Internet, you will notice a new healthy food trend every few days: quinoa, chia seeds, goji berries, lion's mane, ashwagandha. Some of these are even Ayurvedic herbs, yet the wholesale manner in which they are "prescribed" by influencers and enthusiasts alike would make any Ayurvedic doctor get the heebie-jeebies. Without considering the time, place, age, condition, mental state, and digestive state of a person, even the most surefire food rule could be rendered null and void. I can't help thinking about this when I see the little ratings on food packages at the grocery store. Arugula gets an A; cream cheese gets a C. Who decides that? Ayurvedically speaking, if you are in a condition such as I was postpartum, those grades should actually be reversed.

Furthermore, if you are in a state of mental agitation, frustration, or despair, then you might as well give everything an F. According to Ayurveda, food only gets properly digested and absorbed when consumed in a state of calm. (So, if you are having digestive problems that don't seem to be improving no matter how healthy your food is, you may want to start there).

Blindly following other people's food rules means that you may never actually get to the root of the problem. You can continue spending massive amounts of money on supplements, powders, and superfoods and still not have a normal bowel movement the next morning. You can turn your nose up at the cookie platter, dip carrots in hummus instead, yet not lose a single pound, and worse yet, bloat the whole next day. Without an understanding of what type of fuel your body needs at a particular moment, the whole food thing can turn into merely a source of frustration rather than the source of joy and nourishment it is meant to be.

Incorporating the Ayurvedic principle of "like increases like" can be a good starting point. Feeling hot, irritable, and rashy? The chili cheese fries might not be the best option right now. Feeling lethargic and brain foggy? Get yourself some chili, stat. To take it a step further, consider learning more about your body and getting *customized* recommendations about what you need now. Work with an Ayurvedic professional who understands both the science and the demands of your daily life. Get ready to answer questions you haven't been asked since grade school. What is your favorite season? How is your belly feeling? Why did that make you so mad? All of these responses will point to something deeper about your body's needs and will help determine your personal food recommendations. In the meantime, whatever you do, don't follow other people's food rules.

Iman Sheybani is an Ayurvedic health counselor and educator. Since completing her studies in 2021, she has been offering one-on-one consultations, workshops, and courses that equip clients with tools to understand and enhance their digestion based on their body's current needs. Iman lives with her husband and two children in Mallorca, Spain, where she often gathers fruit from nearby trees to prepare her favorite dishes. Mallorca provides the perfect backdrop for experiencing Ayurvedic rituals of renewal and seasonal transition, as showcased by the workshops and events Iman regularly hosts on the island. Learn more about Iman's offerings and sign up for the Iman Ayurveda newsletter to stay updated on upcoming events and insights.

Pinpoint What Your
Reader Craves

Lucinda Halpern

"**A** book for everyone is a book for no one."
When I heard that line early in my career,
it was an "aha!" moment for me. Like so many
writers, I had always thought that the more people your book
claims to reach, the better! But the truth is that most books
start small, with a distinct set of readers.

In the following pages, you'll discover why people buy
books, how to identify your readers, and the three ways your
book can appeal to them. Defining your readership is about
much more than age and gender, although those are important
demographics. Instead, it's about being clear on the purpose
your book delivers.

Focus on Transformation

The best way to understand your reader is to begin by asking: What are readers looking for? Most books are centered around the promise of a transformation. Novels focus on how their characters grow and evolve, though one could argue that the most excellent fiction transforms its characters and readers alike. Universally, I believe readers come to a book for at least one of three reasons:

1. It solves a problem.

2. It delves deep into a fascinating subject.

3. It provides entertainment and delight.

Let's dive into what this means.

Solve a Problem

What top editors have impressed upon me time and again is that for categories like personal development, health, inspirational, and other expertise-driven books, your big idea must address a pain point that readers have and propose a radical solution they haven't seen before. For example, let's say you're an expert in environmental science, and you notice people in the communities where you perform research are having problems with drinking water quality, leading to a higher rate of disease and mortality.

You do more digging and realize there are thousands of communities suffering from a similar problem but very little media coverage about it and no legislative efforts to address it. You have your problem. Now you need to expose this issue for the benefit of the people who are impacted so that readers learn of their problems and get involved.

Often your readers are already aware of a pressing challenge they have and are actively searching for a solution that online fodder or podcasts cannot solve for them decisively. They know they need to take a first step toward improving their circumstances and are willing to spend the price tag of a book for information and guidance that could be life-changing. This was the case for the readers of *Cashing Out*, a personal finance book by my clients Julien and Kiersten Saunders. They knew that Black Americans were fed up with the advice to work hard, make money, save, and invest—advice that appeared far easier for a more advantaged white population. Formerly in corporate roles themselves, they brought a personal viewpoint. The couple wrote *Cashing Out* to teach readers how to achieve financial security, quit high-stress jobs, and retake control of their finances. Their mission was to create more Black millionaires than the world had ever seen. Because they had worked with (and been) underappreciated and underpaid Black Americans for many years, they understood this was a tangible pain point for their reader.

Pain Points for Personal Development Writers

Sometimes I have to talk clients into seeing themselves as "self-help" writers. A writer's first instinct is to tell their life story as memoir. But not only is memoir arguably the most competitive category, a memoir often won't deliver the greatest value or reach as wide a readership if you aren't a known name. You may bristle at the label, but self-help sales are skyrocketing. So many of you have valuable lessons to share. So who's to say a useful book can't also be a work of art? That philosophy is old news. And if you are largely unknown as a writer or on social media, the unique experience and the fresh insights you offer can compensate for a smaller platform.

If you really want to make an impact, you might follow the lead of our student-turned-client Sara McElroy. Initially, her idea was to write a collection of essays about women in the workforce experiencing burnout, especially as it had been exacerbated by the pandemic. Later, she considered memoir. While her tack had a great relatable element (who wasn't burned out by the pandemic?), it was still centrally focused on her own journey. Sara and I had multiple discussions figuring out what the angle should be, and ultimately *Women Who Walk* became a narrative self-help guide that gives women the confidence and tools to leave jobs that no longer serve them. Sara didn't have to remove the personal elements, but she was able to expand her idea to lean into her journalistic interests and create something that would help many women and truly have an impact.

Many nonfiction books, and especially self-help books, boil down to only three categories that are proven, in my experience, to have profound need and urgency. They are:

1. Health

2. Wealth

3. Relationships

Health and wealth are obvious categories. If someone is suffering from burnout, they may be looking for literature on the best practices to try. If someone is starting a new family and struggling to save, a book that promises long-lasting wealth speaks right to the heart of their worry. Stronger relationships make us feel more connected at work and at home.

What I believe unites these categories, what every self-help reader looks for, is freedom. That big-ticket promise—to liberate us from sadness, to elevate us, to untether us from pain—is the transformation from where we are to where we want to be. What I've also discovered about the psychology of book readers is that all of us are, on some level, profoundly lonely. We are looking for our challenges to be seen, our perspective to be heard, or to be touched on some level that we cannot internally provide for ourselves.

Here are some expressions of readers' pain points and the kind of lasting change that you, as an author, can promise. Perhaps you'll recognize your reader and yourself among them.

Reader:

- I've experienced a chronic illness or a loss.

- I do not know how to reach the next level in my job.

- I'm losing my mind as a parent.

- I need to make more money.

- My anxiety is overwhelming my life.

- It is time for me to take control of my health.

- I struggle with relationships and connecting with others.

- I want the key to success that other people seem to have.

Author:

- I can tell you the secrets I've learned for coping with illness or loss.

- You can achieve the career of your dreams.

- There's a toolkit that every parent can use.

- You can gain lasting wealth so long as you know how.

- I'll help you find calm and satisfaction with your life.

- I'll teach you to eat better, live longer, or simply enjoy a healthy lifestyle.

- You will no longer feel alone.

- Here are the mindset and practices of successful people.

What a reader takes away from your book is something agents and publishers need you to answer for them. It should be concrete for you when you conceive of your book, and you need to be able to explain it by the time you pitch it. If your reader is having a challenge of any kind, your book should offer a tangible solution. It's a simple equation of pain to gain.

For more tips and tricks on how to find the book you were born to write, check out *Get Signed: Find an Agent, Land a Book Deal, and Become a Published Author* by Lucinda Halpern.

Lucinda Halpern is a literary agent and the founder of Lucinda Literary, based in New York. She has worked with all major publishers, including Penguin Random House, Simon & Schuster, Macmillan, Hachette, and Scholastic, and currently represents *New York Times* and internationally bestselling authors in the categories of business, personal growth, popular science, narrative nonfiction, memoir, and upmarket fiction. Her classes and coaching programs have been taught to hundreds of writers worldwide and became the inspiration for her new book *Get Signed: Find an Agent, Land a Book Deal, and Become a Published Author* (Hay House; February 6, 2024). Learn more at lucindaliterary.com or download Lucinda's free author training at https://lucindaliterary.lpages.co/free-training/

Go On the Offense with Intellectual Property: Manage It as a Value Driver, Not a Cost Center

Vickie Molenda

T
alk to any intellectual property (IP) attorney, and they can recount many cases in which a client came to them too late. They suffered damage (such as patent infringement or lost market share) when the situation could have been easily prevented. However, the client either didn't know about the potential IP issues or thought it would be too costly to address proactively. They took the defensive approach.

But when business leaders take the offensive approach, they reduce their IP-related legal fees and increase the value of their business. By integrating essential IP considerations into their business plans, they operate under the crucial premise that IP should be viewed and managed as a value driver, not a cost center.

The Predicament of IP Misconceptions

Most business leaders don't fully understand essential IP principles. It's often considered an esoteric subject that can require specialized lawyers to handle, and what is generally known is a vague understanding of patents, trademarks, and copyrights. But that is just the tip of the iceberg for the vast field of IP.

Small and medium-sized enterprises (SMEs) have a lot to juggle: developing and producing the product or service, raising capital, devising a marketing strategy, and hiring. Understandably, they are often very conscious of their financials, constantly raising funds while keeping costs to a minimum. Therefore, the decision is made to put off addressing IP, which is presumed to require expensive attorneys, until absolutely necessary.

SMEs tend to believe in the misconception that addressing IP is cost-prohibitive because "necessity" means responding to a situation: they have an invention they want to patent or a name/logo to trademark, or more dire, a third party is infringing on their IP, they are being accused of infringement, or they need to value their IP for funding or acquisition. In those cases, particularly the latter scenarios, attorney fees can balloon and, understandably, be considered a significant expense. However, minimal investments in time and engagement of attorneys early on can not only add value to the business but also cost substantially less than the legal fees for responding to risks after they emerge.

The other misconception is that SMEs don't need to address IP because they don't have any. On the contrary, almost every business has some form of IP. It may not be a patent or a trademark, but it is still IP, such as trade secrets, that must be considered. Whatever intangible assets the business has that provide an edge over their competitors must be recognized, strengthened, and protected.

Reframing IP: Value Driver vs. Cost Center

The more prudent approach is to view "necessity" as dispelling IP misconceptions and knowing how it can add value to the business and significantly reduce legal fees. Just as business leaders must understand product development, marketing, and fundraising, they must also appreciate how IP can drive business value.

Business leaders who view IP as a value driver can advance business goals through an IP strategy. Depending on those business goals, IP can generate income, provide collateral, block competitors, and/or enhance marketing strategy. With this mindset shift, decisions related to IP are based on the return on investment rather than merely budgeting for a cost center that reacts to legal needs.

During my 15 years as a patent attorney at law firms and Fortune 500 companies, I had many conversations regarding the budget—either the hours we billed the client or the amount being charged by our outside counsel. But other than determining whether patents aligned with research and development goals, we seldom had conversations regarding the overall business goals and the myriad ways IP could advance those goals.

My perspective shift came at a conference discussing the integration of IP, finance, and valuation. Here, I first heard investors stating, "IP should be viewed and managed as a value driver, not a cost center," which is a refreshingly practical viewpoint from a business perspective.

As an IP attorney, I understood the value of IP and the benefits of taking a proactive approach to it, but it was always difficult to get a seat at the table where business decisions were being made. This investor's advice, though, conveyed the importance of IP to business leaders in terms they would appreciate—seeing IP as an active contributor rather than simply a supporting function to be accessed when deemed necessary.

Case Studies: The Cost of Defensive IP Management

The following case studies exemplify common situations that arise when a defensive approach is taken with IP and how an offensive approach would result in added value.

Case Study 1: Inefficient Patent Application Preparation

A client brings an invention to a patent attorney to draft and file a patent application. After telling the attorney about the invention, the client turns over any data from developing the invention and a few related articles. The attorney is then left to draft the application.

As the attorney drafts the application, he pores over all the data provided but inevitably has questions about the invention and/or needs to flesh out possible alternatives to provide the broadest coverage. The attorney starts researching the field of the invention and potential alternatives for each element of the invention, all of which are time billed to the client. The attorney finishes the draft and sends it to the client.

The client reviews the draft and notes questions the attorney embedded in the draft. The questions ask for 1) confirmation of the research and resulting information the attorney added, 2) clarification on any issues the research could not resolve, and 3) availability of specific data that would bolster the application. The client diligently edits the application and answers all the questions for the attorney to revise the draft. As for any additional data, the client does not have the time or funds for further testing. The attorney manages with the information given, and the cycle continues until the final version is completed and filed with a mountain of billable hours and a potentially weaker application. This is a defensive strategy for preparing a patent application.

In an offensive strategy, patent application preparation begins during innovation. The client engages the patent attorney with their idea and preliminary results. The attorney can request the information needed to flesh out the invention, encourage the client to find the white space in the field that may be covered, and suggest data needed to best support the patent application. Since the client is still in the development phase, they have the time and funds to maximize the value of the application.

Case Study 2: Trademark Oversight

An entrepreneur decides on a name and logo for her business. Months later, the business is doing well: sales are better than expected, and the company gains a position in the market. But success also makes the entrepreneur's company a target. The company receives a cease-and-desist letter for trademark infringement due to a similar name.

The entrepreneur acts defensively and hires a lawyer. She learns that she will either 1) have to change the business name and entire branding or 2) fight the accused infringement in litigation. In either case, the entrepreneur will have to spend a significant amount of money and could potentially lose customers due to loss of brand recognition or damage to her reputation for accused trademark infringement.

Alternatively, the entrepreneur takes the offensive approach and pays a minimal fee for conducting a full trademark clearance search before committing to a business name. The search reveals the diminished value of the proposed business name due to existing similar marks. The entrepreneur selects a more valuable alternative and avoids the costly repercussions altogether.

Case Study 3: IP Due Diligence Challenges

Company X is eager to sell a subsidiary and has a potential buyer. Company X hires attorneys for the transaction, including IP attorneys, to review the IP terms. The IP attorneys, however, learn that Company X has not maintained proper records of its registered IP, such as patents, trademarks, and copyrights, much less its unregistered IP rights, such as trade secrets. Now, the IP attorneys must determine which IP is related to the subsidiary Company X wishes to sell and which entity has the rights to that IP.

Under the time crunch and pressure to get the deal done, the IP attorneys not only have to review the contracts, but now they must first identify which assets relate to the subsidiary and determine ownership status. This not only increases the billable time the IP attorneys have to spend on the transaction but also spreads them thin, taking away their ability to concentrate fully on the contract terms.

As the attorneys finalize the IP portfolio assessment, they realize one valuable trade secret is owned by the subsidiary being sold. However, due to the pressure to get the deal done, Company X decides to accept the current terms to sell the subsidiary. By reacting to the opportunity to sell the subsidiary, Company X spends more on the deal for legal fees than expected, the assets of the subsidiary are undervalued, and the contract terms are not as beneficial as they could have been.

In an offensive stance, Company X proactively inventories, determines ownership, and values the IP from conception. When Company X is ready to sell, the subsidiary's value is easily assessed and accounted for in the contract terms, not to mention the fact that countless attorney-billed hours are saved.

Long-Term Benefits & Implementation

Business leaders who invest in understanding offensive IP strategies gain immediate value for their current business and a lifelong skill that benefits all future endeavors. Tying business priorities to IP is fundamental to success—this offensive strategy not only drives business value but also avoids the substantial legal fees associated with reactive, defensive approaches.

To implement this approach, business leaders should develop an IP strategy that aligns all aspects of IP with the other business functions and goals. Only then can SMEs transform IP from a perceived cost center into a value driver for the business.

Vickie Molenda brings over two decades of experience in innovation to help businesses develop a proactive intellectual property strategy. As a patent attorney with a research science background, Vickie managed biopharmaceutical patent portfolios for various clients at large law firms before transitioning to in-house counsel roles at Fortune 500 companies, where she supported product development and collaborations. Vickie founded Immescherable Consulting LLC to provide essential methods for businesses to implement an IP strategy that maximizes the value of their intellectual property and effectively collaborates with IP counsel.

To receive her checklist for developing an IP strategy, visit www.immescherable.com/free-IP-strategy-checklist.

Section 5:
Financial
Wellbeing & Security

Come to the
Conversation Curious

Emily Scott

In an interview about my practice—understanding your money story and its role in your relationships and decision-making—I was asked, "Which conversation should I approach with curiosity?" Without hesitation, I answered, "Every single one. The journey begins with yourself and then includes others. There is so much to learn." Until you are clear about your own narrative, all other conversations risk unsatisfactory results. The beauty of this approach is how quickly curiosity about money expands to enrich all other aspects of your life.

Our individual money stories—unique as our fingerprints—affect our decision-making, our relationships, our peace of mind, and our clarity of purpose. Though we often treat money as merely a practical tool, it carries deep emotional significance that shapes our lives in ways we may not fully understand.

We know that humans are complex beings and, as such, there is far more to understand about our individuality than simple categorizations allow. That complexity also exists in the money realm. While we focus on the tactical—spending, saving, taxes, planning—we rarely discuss money's emotional dimension. Yet research confirms that emotions drive our financial decisions. We make choices that profoundly affect our lives without comprehending the deeper forces at work.

Until you clearly understand your emotional relationship with money, every other money conversation—whether with a partner, family member, or financial advisor—will be limited or potentially fraught with conflict.

That's why my first piece of advice to every client is simple: "Come to the conversation curious." Curiosity must begin internally, examining your own narratives before extending outward to productive conversations with others. Opening your mind and activating your curiosity gives you the opportunity to accept that something may be your belief rather than truth, that your personal narratives may be both helping and getting in your way, and that your fears may be creating myths and barriers that hinder your goals and relationships.

Curiosity becomes the bridge that allows us to explore both the practical and emotional dimensions of our relationship with money. Without it, we remain stuck in patterns we don't understand. This is the essence of curiosity: embracing the unknown, recognizing that our stories evolve, and welcoming the transformative power of growth and change.

What is Your Money Story?

What is your money story? It is all the messages you have received—implicitly and explicitly—since you were first aware of what money actually is. Starting in the home, with more information pouring in from outside sources, including school, houses of worship, media, and so forth. Your culture and ethnicity also shape these messages. The gender messages start early. Girls are told, "Save your babysitting money for something you really want," while boys are taught, "Hold on to those baseball cards; they will be worth something one day." You get the drift.

These early messages form the foundation of how we relate to money throughout our lives. They operate below the level of conscious awareness yet drive some of our most important decisions.

From Uncertainty to Self-Trust

Dr. Julia DiGangi, a neuropsychologist, is an expert in the connection between our brains, emotions, and relationships. She explains that the human brain is allergic to uncertainty, and seeking external certainty only increases anxiety. Dr. DiGangi offers that the opposite of uncertainty is not certainty, but self-trust. The path to self-trust? Learning about your emotions to transform your emotional pain into emotional power.

As I say—become friends with your emotions. At some point, you gain the wisdom of your essence and can more easily distinguish between self-trust and noise.

Why This Matters: The Diverse Impact of Money Stories

Business partners disagreeing on how to invest in their business, a couple fighting over finances, a recent widow transitioning into singlehood, a family entering the world of philanthropy, someone who recently came into a financial windfall, and parents concerned about raising entitled children—all of these clients needed to learn about the money stories they carry and how those emotions affect their tangible decisions about money. Their answers differ because each person's history and circumstances are unique.

Learning about your money story is challenging because many of us were taught never to discuss money. This taboo makes it difficult to recognize that money has an emotional dimension at all, let alone to understand how it shapes our lives.

If you have ever talked to a financial advisor, you were probably asked, "What is your risk tolerance?" I submit that the more relevant inquiry is, "How did your risk tolerance come to be?" This invites exploration of your money story and its critical underpinnings. Now you and your advisor have information to discuss that is far more relevant to addressing your specific needs.

This curiosity-based approach leads to knowledge expansion, authentic conversations, consensus-building, and solutions that honor the complexity of each person's relationship with money. Given that our money stories are individually unique, learning yours is the catalyst to discovering what works well for you and what inhibits achieving your goals.

The "And" Approach: Embracing Both Emotion and Practicality

Exploring the development of your money story is not an "either/or" situation. This is an "and." You must understand your emotions and identify the driving forces. In this way, you seek to understand what's going on inside yourself. As you gain knowledge of your essence, there is newfound peace of mind and clarity when you're making decisions about any aspect of your money and why these choices matter. Your thought process changes, and with that, so do your beliefs and behaviors. Clients describe it as a sense of freedom. This understanding can extend to other aspects of your life. With that experience, it follows that everything around you gets evaluated in much the same light. That's when the *earth shift* begins.

The Core Philosophy: Being Seen, Heard, and Valued

One of my core principles is a belief that people need to be seen, be heard, and know that they matter. People are not a target, not a commodity. Asking questions is an outgrowth of this philosophy. This approach guides us into unfamiliar territory—beyond taboos and into moments of clarity. To reach your "North Star," you must spend time on your journey. The rush to the destination assumes that you are clear about the destination and that you know all there is to know about your journey. This opens you up to second-guessing, decision-making anxiety, confrontation, and results that may not serve you well. Simply put, it is the journey *and* the destination.

Curiosity In Action

How does this layer of curiosity around one's money story manifest? Some examples:

- **A couple's financial conversations were so tense that they started avoiding them, which only led to more arguments.** When we unpacked their individual money stories, we found quite different perspectives. The husband grew up in a feast/famine environment and believed that pattern would continue and all would be fine. The wife grew up with her grandparents, who were conservative in their spending and believed in saving for the unknown. This wasn't a question of someone being a "spender" and someone being a "cheapskate." Finding the root cause of their different approaches allowed for robust conversations about how to proceed without confrontation.

- **Two lawyers started a practice that was growing nicely. One wanted to spend money on promoting their practice. The other did not, as the tangible return was not obvious to them.** A review of their money stories showed the root cause of their different perspectives. One was raised with a philosophy of "spend to enjoy." The second was a first-generation American and learned "every penny is precious." Making matters worse, after many heated discussions, the first lawyer would say, "Well, I'll just pay for it," and then resent that his generosity was not warmly received. His partner felt like his perspective didn't matter, that their equal partnership was not so equal after all. With their emotional intelligence increased, their ability to move forward in alignment and grow their business became a much smoother process.

- **A client inherited a large sum of money and felt conflicted about what to do.** Everyone had an opinion—his financial advisor, accountant, lawyer, friends, and family. Through a series of conversations and exercises, including work around his values, thoughts about his legacy, and his money story, we put together a potential plan aligned with his values. With that draft, he could then work with his advisors on how to execute the plan and also learn what the benefits/consequences would be. The conversations were the perfect combination of technical and personal.

• **After a decade of being single, a client was about to remarry.** Her first husband was very controlling around money and was not generous with the divorce settlement. Her soon-to-be husband was far wealthier than she was and seemed to be as equally controlling about money as her first husband. Her fear of not having any say about their money decisions and being in a financially dire situation yet again was affecting her well-being. Included in our work was differentiating between the anxieties that clouded her perspective and her instincts that served her well. She was able to sit down with her fiancé and create a money partnership that met both of their needs.

The Ripple Effect of Curiosity

When you approach your money story with curiosity, the benefits extend far beyond your finances. Think of this as the foundation of creating your personal mission statement. The self-awareness you gain transforms how you show up in all areas of life. You begin living more intentionally, making decisions aligned with your true values rather than unconscious patterns.

Curiosity is not merely a starting point—it's a continuous practice that allows your money story to evolve as you grow. The question isn't "What's your money story?" but rather "How are you allowing your money story to evolve through curiosity?" The question isn't only "Can I afford it?" but rather "Can I afford it **and** is this the way I want my money to represent who I am?" This approach on your journey toward your "North Star" brings you alignment with who you truly are.

Emily Scott guides clients in learning how their money story affects their personal and professional financial decision-making, communication, and relationships. With no assets under management, her focus is on the clients' clarity and peace of mind. Ms. Scott has over 40 years of experience in investing, family office management, philanthropy, and legacy planning. Emily presented at TED on philanthropy and has contributed to media on women in transition, struggles with wealth, couples navigating their differences, and philanthropic perspectives. She has received accolades for her unique approach and candor. She holds an MBA from Cornell University and a BA from Simmons College, and she is a member of The Sudden Money Institute and Forward Global.

Transform your relationship with money by understanding your unique money story at emilyscottand.com, where Emily Scott helps clients gain clarity and peace of mind around financial decisions.

Beyond the Golden Cage

Dr. Jeanette Denker

Beauty was passed down to me through a lineage of gorgeous women—fashion models. I often wondered if beauty contributed to their heartbreak. They all seemed to choose the wrong men: men who seemed loving and went above and beyond to show their care in the beginning but became their biggest nightmare, often years later.

No choice these women made seemed to lead to a positive outcome. Staying in the relationship left them increasingly exhausted. No matter how much they gave or how perfect they tried to be for their partner, it was never enough. He drew them in like a spell, and everything moved so quickly— from engagement to a perfect wedding and a baby or several. Yet, they ended up trapped, like a bird in a golden cage.

Despite all that I witnessed, I followed the same flight pattern.

By the time you realize you're trapped, you understand there's nothing you could ever be, do, or give to the man you called the love of your life that would restore what once was. Day by day, it only gets worse as he gains more power, keeping you trapped through isolation, control, and manipulation. This leads to great despair and physical illness. Your body, once your currency, shows signs of years of betrayal. You're made to feel responsible: "You don't pay enough attention to me," he says. "You're too focused on the children," "You refuse to have threesomes to spice up our sex life, which is why I had to look elsewhere," or "You're too fat and not as attractive and energetic as when I first met you. Maybe you should see a nutritionist." OK, the last two statements may have been lobbed at me alone.

You understand the rules, just as the women of my family had. Always look like a model, even if you just gave birth. "You are sitting at home doing nothing while I work hard to provide for our family; show some appreciation." "It's your fault I cheated on you because you didn't spend enough time with me, and I had to go out to clubs on the weekends by myself." "If you only paid more attention to me, you wouldn't force me to make these decisions." "I just need to feel loved and cared for; that's what every man wants. If he doesn't get it from his wife, he will look for it elsewhere." "Wipe those tears; I should be the one crying for how much you have hurt me by making the kids a priority over me."

The women in my family are not the only ones who have fallen into this trap. I see you everywhere, and I know what happens next.

When it seems it cannot get any worse, as you find out about yet another girlfriend—or worse, your children do—you finally get the courage to file for divorce. You have no idea that this very moment of courage will turn what used to be the love of your life into a monster. A demon that will go to great lengths to destroy you and everyone around you, even if that includes his own children.

You must prepare strategically and seek professional psychological support before attempting to leave a high-conflict marriage with a powerful, controlling partner. That's my advice to you.

The financial abuse will only increase, matching the level of intensity as when you first fell in love. You will find yourself blocked from all financial accounts. You and the children may be living in a home he is actively driving toward foreclosure because you no longer want him there. You might live in a castle on the beach and drive a luxurious car, only to discover he has canceled your car insurance or finds it entertaining to cut off the electricity, internet, or water supply, or cancel food deliveries, just to ensure you feel the impact of his absence in your life.

He wants you to understand that the cheating, his strip club visits, his absence at home, and his raging anger toward you or your children were just a walk in the garden compared to what lies ahead now.

Why? Because he knows the legal system. He understands that it is painfully slow, and he has an army of attorneys who can prolong any hearing far beyond what you can endure.

In his mind, you deserve nothing because you dared to decide you no longer want to be with him. He is unafraid, believing that his wealth can buy anyone and anything, placing him above the law. His lack of empathy fuels his eagerness to break you down so he can continue to control you, making you agree to anything just so the children can have a good meal or experience the smallest semblance of what used to be a normal childhood.

Every day, women with powerful husbands are broken down as a form of punishment. The coercive power of affluent and recognized men shows no mercy. The couple that outsiders perceive as having it all often reveals a starkly different reality. Those beautiful couples on the front page of the paper or on the movie screens.

Who would ever think that someone living in a multi-million-dollar mansion would struggle to afford diapers, gas, or food for their children?

Who would believe they could be financially starved and barred from access to their own accounts, with no friends or family to help—an isolation systematically enforced over years of marriage?

Who would think that even if you could ask for help, you wouldn't? Deeply ashamed of your situation, you find it incredibly difficult to seek assistance, having only learned how to help others and organize charity work, never acquiring the skills to ask for help for yourself.

So, when you find yourself in a dangerous situation with a once charming and powerful man, it may be time to start seeing a psychologist—one who understands the world of the affluent. You are like a bird in a golden cage, desperately needing strategic planning and solution-focused therapy before making your first move and consulting a family attorney.

Don't wait too long to have strategic, solution-focused sessions with a professional who understands your fears and shame. This support can help you remain strong and steady as you rebuild your sense of self and carefully plan your exit. You cannot allow him to harm you or the children any longer.

You need to learn how to stay calm in any situation so you can be the best mom for your children. You may not know what lies ahead, and neither option seems like a winning one. You might question whether you have the courage and strength to file for divorce, but you also realize you can no longer continue in this toxic marriage while pretending to be a happy family. Each day you stay only fragments you further.

Often, I reflect on the past and ask myself what I would have done differently. Based on what I know now, evaluating my own high-conflict divorce as well as those of the women I've served in the role of psychologist or narcissistic abuse-awareness coach, here is the most valuable advice I can give you:

1. No matter how horrible, hopeless, and scary your situation may seem, as long as you do not give up or give in, you will find a solution and emerge more resilient in the end. There is a life experience and extraordinary strength you gain when faced with the most difficult times in your life.

2. Whatever money you saved to get through the divorce, and whatever relief you thought the judge would order for you, you will likely run out sooner than you think. Have a backup plan. Ensure you know someone who can lend you money, maintain strong credit, and consider using credit cards or taking out loans if the court process takes too long.

3. The moment you start thinking about leaving, begin collecting gift cards for groceries or any shops you frequently visit for yourself and your children. These will be your silver lining when you least expect it.

4. You may be mistaken about who your best friends or good friends are while you are married. Prepare yourself for the possibility that once you file for divorce, those same people who were there for years, ready to join every party or event you organized, may suddenly disappear or express discomfort about getting involved. Embrace these "losses" and remain open to making new, amazing friends for life.

5. If you are at the very beginning of your journey and just starting to think about divorce, please educate yourself about your household finances. Just because you have a housekeeper working 40 hours a week and a babysitter who handles shopping for the home, along with receiving $1,000 in cash weekly for your and your children's needs, does not mean that you will have that support once you initiate the divorce process.

6. Before you leave your marriage, ask questions, investigate, and understand every investment account, retirement account, bank account, and business transaction. Do not trust blindly that your husband will take care of you and your children as he promised. Know your household and personal expenses for yourself and your children before relying on your husband to tell the truth.

7. Always think of your children first; this will give you the strength to keep moving forward.

Having the best attorney for your specific case is important, but it may be second to having a strong, solution-focused psychologist and coach who can guide you with high confidentiality and help you rebuild each time you feel broken.

Dr. Jeanette Denker is a dedicated advocate for peace and resilience, committed to guiding individuals from the shadows of narcissistic and financial abuse toward a brighter, empowered future. Her firsthand experience with the complexities of relationships with powerful figures has given her a deep understanding of the emotional turmoil her clients face. With remarkable insight and strategic expertise, she helps her clients reclaim their power and rebuild their self-esteem and confidence. Here is her unique offer: the first ten readers will receive a complimentary two-hour initial session. Simply scan the QR code below to begin reclaiming your power.